1957 Chevrolet Bel Air

Cruising Through Time

Todd Bandel

ISBN: 978-1-970265-00-2

DEDICATION

To Howard Fox,
Thanks for lighting the spark that made this book possible. Your
inspiration and support mean the world to me!

Content

ACKNOWLEDGEMENT

i

CHAPTER ONE

American Icon: Introduction to the '57 Bel Air Phenomenon　　1

Chapter Two

Detroit's Masterpiece: The Birth and Design Evolution of the '57 Bel Air　　13

Chapter Three

Tailfins and Chrome: Jet Age Aesthetics and Styling Innovations　　29

Chapter Four

TUnder the Hood: Powertrains, Engineering, and Technical Specifications　　45

Chapter Five

Factory to Showroom: Production Processes and Model Variations　　65

Chapter Six

The Tri-Five Family: Comparing the '57 to its '55 and '56 Siblings　　81

Chapter Seven

Cultural Milestone: The Bel Air in 1950s American Society　　97

Chapter Eight

Screen and Sound: The Bel Air in Film, Television, and Music　　115

Chapter Nine

Preservation of a Legacy: Restoration Fundamentals and Best Practices　　135

Chapter Ten

Collector Chronicles: Personal Stories from Owners and Restorers　　151

Chapter Eleven

Investment on Wheels: Valuation, Auction Trends, and Market Analysis　　173

Chapter Twelve

Bel Air Nation: Clubs, Shows, and a Community of Enthusiasts　　191

ACKNOWLEDGMENTS

I want to express my deepest gratitude to my father for introducing me to the exhilarating world of automotive racing. Your passion for cars and dedication to the sport have inspired me.

From the first time you took me to a race track, I was captivated by the power and precision of the machines, as well as the skill required to master them.

Your guidance and support have fueled my interest and enthusiasm, making every moment in this thrilling world more meaningful. Thank you for sharing this incredible journey with me and for being such a pivotal influence in my life.

Chapter 1: American Icon: Introduction to the '57 Bel Air Phenomenon

Section 1.1: Defining an Era: The '57 Bel Air in Historical Context

The 1957 Chevrolet Bel Air emerged during a transformative period in American history, when the nation was experiencing unprecedented economic prosperity following the hardships of World War II. The post-war boom had fundamentally altered the American landscape, with suburban sprawl redefining cities and the automobile becoming not just a luxury but a necessity for the modern American family.

By the mid-1950s, America's love affair with the automobile had reached new heights. The wartime rationing of materials and production restrictions were distant memories as automakers competed vigorously in a market hungry for bigger, faster, and more stylish vehicles. The American highway system was expanding under President Eisenhower's Federal-Aid Highway Act of 1956, creating an infrastructure that would forever change how Americans lived, worked, and traveled. This nationwide development fueled demand for automobiles that could handle longer distances with greater comfort.

Against this backdrop of industrial might and consumer optimism, Chevrolet introduced the 1957 Bel Air, a car perfectly calibrated to capture the spirit of its time. The automotive boom had shifted from merely fulfilling pent-up demand to providing vehicles that expressed individuality and status. Americans weren't just buying transportation; they were purchasing dreams on wheels, and few dreams were as captivating as the '57 Bel Air.

What distinguished this particular model year was its impeccable timing. Arriving just as television was becoming commonplace in American homes and rock 'n' roll was transforming popular music, the '57 Bel Air represented the convergence of technological advancement and cultural expression. Its design reflected America's newfound confidence and optimism, a nation looking toward a future of boundless possibilities, where even the family car could be a work of art.

The automotive boom that gave birth to the '57 Bel Air was more than an economic phenomenon; it was a cultural movement that redefined American identity. As families gathered in driveways to admire their new purchases and teenagers cruised main streets in gleaming Chevrolets, the automobile, notably the Bel Air, became woven into the fabric of American life, a symbol of achievement as potent as a home in the suburbs or a television in the living room.

Section 1.2: How the Bel Air embodied American prosperity and optimism

The 1957 Chevrolet Bel Air didn't merely represent a mode of transportation; it emerged as the rolling embodiment of American prosperity and unbridled optimism that characterized the mid-1950s.

1957 Chevrolet Bel Air: Cruising Through Time

Coming nearly a decade after World War II's conclusion, the Bel Air arrived at a moment when the United States had firmly established itself as a global economic powerhouse, with a burgeoning middle class enjoying unprecedented access to consumer goods and homeownership.

The Bel Air's generous proportions, abundant chrome, and distinctive tail fins perfectly encapsulated the national mood of confidence and forward momentum. In an era when bigger was unquestionably better, the Bel Air delivered size and presence in abundance, yet remained attainable for middle-class families, a perfect synthesis of aspiration and accessibility. Its design language spoke of aerospace influences and jet-age technology, mirroring America's fascination with conquering new frontiers, both on Earth and beyond.

For many families, the purchase of a Bel Air represented the achievement of the "American Dream", a tangible symbol that hard work and determination had paid off. Parked in the driveway of a newly constructed suburban home, the Bel Air completed the picture of post-war prosperity that millions of Americans were eager to claim as their own. The car's available options, power steering, power brakes, air conditioning, and an automatic transmission provided luxuries that would have seemed unimaginable to previous generations.

The Bel Air's bold color combinations, including vibrant two-tone treatments, reflected the nation's exuberant mood. No longer constrained by wartime austerity or rationing, Americans embraced Bel Air's cheerful palette as an expression of newfound freedom and optimism. Even its advertising emphasized not just transportation but lifestyle, showing happy families enjoying leisure activities made possible by their sleek new Chevrolet.

As suburban developments expanded and the interstate highway system began transforming the landscape, the Bel Air promised the freedom to explore a nation whose boundaries seemed to grow with each passing year. It was the perfect vehicle for Sunday drives, family vacations, and cruising to drive-in theaters and restaurants, all central components of America's new leisure-oriented lifestyle.

Perhaps most significantly, the '57 Bel Air represented a moment of American industrial dominance and creative confidence, a time when American design and manufacturing were setting global standards rather than following them. The car's unapologetic styling announced that America had moved beyond the functional focus of the war years and was embracing a bold new aesthetic that celebrated abundance, technological progress, and unlimited horizons.

In this way, the 1957 Bel Air wasn't just a product of its time; it helped define its time, becoming both a mirror reflecting American prosperity and a canvas upon which Americans projected their optimistic vision of the future.

Section 1.3: The Cultural Backdrop of 1957: Music, Fashion, and Technology

The '57 Bel Air didn't emerge in a vacuum; it was both a product and a reflection of a vibrant cultural moment in American history. The year 1957 stood at a pivotal crossroads between post-war conservatism and the revolutionary changes that would define the 1960s.

In the realm of music, rock and roll was reaching its first commercial peak. Elvis Presley had become a household name, appearing on The Ed Sullivan Show and releasing hits like "Jailhouse Rock" and "All Shook Up." Meanwhile, artists like Buddy Holly, Chuck Berry, and Little Richard were transforming the American

4

soundscape. The car radio, standard equipment in the Bel Air, became the delivery mechanism for this cultural revolution, with teenagers cruising Main Streets across America with their windows down and music blaring.

Fashion in 1957 remained relatively conservative compared to what would follow, yet changes were brewing. Men still favored suits for formal occasions, but casual wear was gaining acceptance. Women's fashion featured the full-skirted silhouettes popularized by Christian Dior's "New Look," with tiny waists and expansive petticoats that seemed to mirror the wide, substantial stance of cars like the Bel Air. Pastel colors dominated both clothing and automotive design, with turquoise, coral, and butter yellow appearing on everything from kitchen appliances to the Bel Air's optional two-tone paint schemes.

Technologically, America was racing into the future. Just months before the '57 Bel Air debuted, the Space Age officially began when the Soviet Union launched Sputnik in October 1957, igniting the space race and America's fascination with all things futuristic. Television was becoming ubiquitous in American homes, with nearly 85% of households owning a set by 1957. Programs like "I Love Lucy" and "The Honeymooners" shaped national conversations and consumer desires.

Consumer culture was in full bloom, with suburban expansion creating new markets for household appliances and leisure goods. The prosperity that enabled families to purchase a new Bel Air also allowed them to furnish their new ranch-style homes with appliances such as dishwashers, refrigerators, and vacuum cleaners. Credit was increasingly available, making luxury purchases more accessible to the middle class.

This was also the era of the emerging interstate highway system, which was signed into law by President Eisenhower just a year earlier, in 1956. Americans were becoming increasingly mobile, and the automobile played a central role in this newfound freedom. Weekend drives, road trips, and the rise of drive-in movies, restaurants, and shopping centers all contributed to a culture where the automobile was not just a means of transportation but a lifestyle accessory.

In this context, the 1957 Bel Air wasn't merely a means of transportation; it was a vessel for American dreams and aspirations. Its forward-looking design, with elements reminiscent of jet aircraft and rockets, resonated perfectly with a nation looking toward a promising future while enjoying unprecedented prosperity in the present. The car's styling captured the optimistic spirit of the times, making it not just a product of 1957's cultural moment but one of its most enduring symbols.

Section 1.4: The Bel Air Within Chevrolet's Hierarchy

Within Chevrolet's carefully structured product lineup of 1957, the Bel Air represented the pinnacle of the brand's offerings. It stood as the crown jewel in a three-tiered hierarchy that included the entry-level 150 series and the mid-range 210 series. This stratification allowed Chevrolet to appeal to multiple market segments while maintaining a clear aspirational ladder for consumers.

The base 150 series, often purchased by fleet operators and budget-conscious buyers, offered Chevrolet reliability without the frills. It's plain trim and limited options kept the price accessible, but its utilitarian nature was evident in both its appearance and marketing. Moving up to the 210 series, buyers found more chrome trim, better upholstery, and additional comfort features that signaled a step above basic transportation.

The Bel Air, however, represented Chevrolet's vision of attainable luxury. With its price ranging from approximately $2,100 for a base sedan to nearly $2,800 for a well-equipped convertible, the Bel Air positioned itself as an aspirational yet realistic purchase for

America's growing middle class. This pricing strategy placed it within reach of successful blue-collar workers, mid-level managers, and small business owners who wanted to showcase their prosperity without venturing into the territory of truly premium brands.

Demographically, Bel Air owners typically represented successful middle-class Americans in their 30s and 40s, often with young families. Marketing materials frequently depicted the Bel Air in suburban settings, reinforcing its association with the American dream of homeownership and upward mobility. These buyers were willing to pay the premium over the 150 and 210 series to enjoy distinctive styling touches, such as the model's signature side trim, plush interiors, and comprehensive feature sets.

Within General Motors' broader ecosystem, the Bel Air occupied a strategic position. It sat below Oldsmobile, Buick, and Cadillac in the corporate hierarchy, but offered styling and features that sometimes rivaled those of its more expensive siblings. This positioning occasionally created tension within GM, as the Bel Air's combination of style, performance, and value proposition sometimes threatened to cannibalize sales from Oldsmobile and Buick models.

The 1957 Buick Special, for instance, started at nearly $700 more than the comparable Bel Air, yet didn't necessarily offer $700 more value in the eyes of many consumers. Similarly, the Oldsmobile 88 commanded a significant premium despite sharing many basic engineering principles with its Chevrolet cousin. The Bel Air's value proposition was so strong that it occasionally forced GM's higher divisions to justify their premium pricing through more distinctive styling, additional features, or marketing that emphasized prestige rather than practical benefits.

This delicate balancing act within GM's hierarchy highlighted the Bel Air's exceptional position as a car that delivered premium experiences without a premium price tag. Its ability to satisfy aspirational desires while maintaining practical affordability is one of the key factors in its enduring appeal and eventual iconic status in American automotive history.

Section 1.5: From Status Symbol to Cultural Icon

The journey of the 1957 Chevrolet Bel Air from showroom sensation to cultural touchstone reveals much about American automotive heritage and our relationship with iconic design. When the Bel Air first graced American driveways in the late 1950s, ownership represented achievement of the American dream. These weren't merely transportation; they were status symbols announcing one's arrival in middle-class prosperity.

Initial owners experienced the Bel Air as the pinnacle of attainable luxury. With its optional power steering, brakes, windows, and seats, the Bel Air delivered a taste of high-end comfort previously reserved for premium brands. Families proudly parked their gleaming new Chevrolets in driveways, taking Sunday drives and creating memories that would later fuel nostalgia for the era. The car was a participant in significant life moments, proms, weddings, and family vacations, embedding itself in the personal histories of countless Americans.

As the 1960s arrived, the '57 Bel Air began its transition from contemporary transportation to something more meaningful. While newer models pushed boundaries of power and styling, the Bel Air's distinctive silhouette remained instantly recognizable. First-generation owners might have traded up for newer models, but many held onto their '57s out of attachment or practicality. Meanwhile, these cars became affordable entries into car culture for a younger generation, particularly as hot rodding culture expanded. Teenagers and young adults who couldn't afford a new GTO or Mustang could acquire a used Bel Air and modify it, inadvertently preserving many examples that might otherwise have been scrapped.

1957 Chevrolet Bel Air: Cruising Through Time

The 1970s marked a pivotal turning point in Bel Air's cultural trajectory. Amidst fuel shortages and the dominance of compact imports, the Bel Air stood as a reminder of a different America, one characterized by confidence, expansiveness, and chrome-laden exuberance. The stark contrast between new angular, fuel-efficient designs and the Bel Air's flowing lines and substantial presence triggered a wave of nostalgia. This period also saw the emergence of dedicated classic car publications, shows, and clubs, with the '57 Chevy frequently featured as the quintessential American classic.

By the 1980s, the transformation was complete. Hollywood embraced the '57 Bel Air as visual shorthand for the 1950s era, featuring it prominently in films like "American Graffiti," "Diner," and later "The Right Stuff." Television shows and music videos similarly adopted the car as an instantly recognizable symbol of mid-century America. Collectors began restoring these vehicles not just for personal enjoyment but as investments, recognizing their cultural significance and rising value.

The advent of dedicated automotive television programming in the 1990s and 2000s further cemented the Bel Air's iconic status. Restoration shows frequently featured '57 Chevys, introducing new generations to their appeal. Simultaneously, auction prices climbed steadily, with pristine examples commanding six-figure sums, far from their original $2,400 price tag.

What distinguishes the '57 Bel Air's journey is its broad appeal across generations. Unlike many classics that appeal primarily to those who remember them when new, the Bel Air continues to attract enthusiasts born decades after its production ended. It has achieved what few automobiles have: transcending its original purpose to become a cultural artifact, an artistic achievement, and a rolling repository of American optimism during a defining historical moment.

Section 1.6: Enduring Appeal: Why the '57 Stands Above Other Classics

The 1957 Chevrolet Bel Air's enduring appeal goes beyond mere nostalgia; it represents a perfect convergence of design brilliance, cultural timing, and engineering prowess that few automobiles have ever achieved. What separates the '57 Bel Air from countless other classic cars is its timeless design language. While many vehicles from the 1950s appear exaggerated or dated by today's standards, the Bel Air's proportions maintain a remarkable balance.

Its sweeping lines and thoughtful detailing create a visual harmony that resonates across generations. The iconic tailfins, while decidedly of their era, were executed with such restraint and integration into the overall design that they enhance rather than dominate the car's silhouette. This design restraint has allowed the Bel Air to age gracefully, appearing less a caricature of the 1950s and more a timeless expression of automotive beauty.

The Bel Air also benefited from impeccable timing within American culture. It arrived at the peak of America's post-war confidence, when optimism about the future merged with economic prosperity. The car embodied the nation's self-image, bold yet sophisticated, powerful yet accessible. Unlike luxury vehicles that remained out of reach for most Americans, or economy cars that lacked prestige, the Bel Air struck the perfect balance as an attainable status symbol. Its presence in driveways across America cemented its place in the collective memory of multiple generations.

Engineering innovations further strengthened Bel Air's lasting appeal. The introduction of the optional fuel-injected 283 cubic inch V8 engine, capable of producing one horsepower per cubic inch, was revolutionary for a mass-produced automobile. This technical achievement gave the Bel Air performance credentials to match its stylish appearance, creating a dual legacy of both beauty and capability. The car's solid construction and relatively straightforward mechanical design have also contributed to its longevity, allowing many examples to survive into the present day and remain serviceable decades after production.

The cultural timing, aesthetic achievement, and mechanical innovation created a perfect storm that elevated the '57 Bel Air beyond being merely another attractive automobile. It became a rolling embodiment of American optimism, the four-wheeled manifestation of a specific moment in time when style, technology, and national confidence aligned. This combination of factors explains why, among thousands of models produced throughout automotive history, the '57 Bel Air continues to stand out as an enduring icon.

As we'll explore throughout this book, the legacy of the 1957 Chevrolet Bel Air extends far beyond its initial production run. Its influence can be seen in subsequent automotive designs, its presence in popular culture remains strong, and its status as one of the most desirable collector cars continues undiminished after more than six decades. The Bel Air isn't merely a survivor of its era; it's a timeless ambassador that continues to captivate new generations of enthusiasts who weren't even born when it first graced American highways.

Section 1.7: The 1957 Chevrolet Bel Air, A Timeless Icon of American Optimism

The 1957 Chevrolet Bel Air stands as more than just a classic automobile; it represents a singular moment in American cultural history where design, engineering, and societal optimism converged to create something truly extraordinary. Throughout this chapter, we've explored how the Bel Air emerged during a prosperous post-war period when American automakers were reaching new heights of both innovation and influence. The car's immediate reception, from glowing media reviews to strong dealership performance, demonstrated its contemporary appeal. At the same time, its placement at the top of Chevrolet's lineup positioned it as an attainable luxury for middle-class Americans.

We've seen how Harley Earl's forward-thinking design philosophy created a vehicle that balanced aesthetic beauty with practical functionality, establishing styling cues that would influence automotive design for decades to come. The Bel Air's journey from showroom star to cultural icon wasn't immediate but evolved organically as the car came to symbolize the optimism and prosperity of its era. What truly distinguishes the '57 Bel Air from countless other classic cars is its perfect alignment of inspired design, solid engineering, and cultural significance, a combination that continues to resonate with enthusiasts and casual observers alike.

As we move into Chapter 2, we'll take a deeper dive into the fascinating design and development process that brought the '57 Bel Air to life. We'll explore the competitive landscape that shaped Chevrolet's decision-making, meet the key personalities who championed the project, and examine the evolution from initial concept sketches to the final production model. The next chapter reveals how General Motors' immense resources and talent pool were harnessed to create what would become not just a successful product, but an enduring symbol of American automotive excellence.

Chapter 2: Detroit's Masterpiece: The Birth and Design Evolution of the '57 Bel Air

Section 2.1: Design Evolution from Previous Models: The Tri-Five Progression

The 1957 Chevrolet Bel Air represented the culmination of what would later be called the "Tri-Five" era, a three-year production run from 1955 to 1957 that would forever change American automotive design. This progression wasn't merely coincidental but rather a carefully orchestrated evolution that balanced innovation with brand continuity.

The '55 Chevy had initiated a bold departure from previous models with its clean, modern lines and distinctive front end. It introduced a revolutionary chassis and the small-block V8 engine that would become legendary. When examining the transition to the '56 model, one notes subtle refinements rather than radical changes: a full-width grille replaced the Ferrari-inspired design of the '55, and the side trim was revised to accommodate more elaborate two-tone paint schemes.

1957 Chevrolet Bel Air: Cruising Through Time

The '57 Bel Air, however, while clearly related to its predecessors, made several significant leaps forward. It retained the bare body shell and 115-inch wheelbase of the previous models, providing manufacturing efficiency and brand recognition. The roofline maintained the graceful, flowing shape that had become a Chevrolet signature, though with subtle refinements. Similarly, the wraparound windshield, a modernist touch introduced in the '55, was preserved but slightly modified for improved visibility and aesthetics.

Interior layouts also showed evolutionary consistency. The basic dashboard arrangement, with its twin-cove design, remained recognizable across all three years. However, the '57 model introduced a more horizontal emphasis to create a greater sense of width and space. The distinctive ribbed stainless steel dashboard and door panel inserts, elements that had become Bel Air signatures, were retained but refined.

Where the '57 deliberately departed from its predecessors was in its more dramatic styling elements. The front end underwent a comprehensive redesign, adopting a wider, lower appearance with a massive bumper/grille combination that gave the car a more substantial presence. The hood was flattened and extended forward, creating a longer profile that enhanced the car's luxury appeal.

Most dramatically, the rear treatment of the '57 introduced pronounced tailfins, far more prominent than the modest suggestions found on the '55 and '56 models. These fins, capped with distinctive chrome trim and housing revolutionary twin bullet taillights on each side, became the car's most identifiable feature and represented the clearest break from previous designs.

The '57 also featured more elaborate ornamentation throughout, with additional chrome accents along the body sides and hood. The iconic side trim, a distinguishing feature across the Tri-Five lineup, evolved from the straight spear of the '55 to the more elaborate, angled treatment of the '57, creating opportunities for more complex two-tone paint arrangements.

This balanced approach to design evolution, maintaining core elements while introducing sufficient novelty, proved masterful. It allowed Chevrolet to capitalize on the success of previous models while offering consumers something fresh and exciting, a strategy that would help the '57 Bel Air transcend its predecessors to become the most enduring symbol of the entire Tri-Five generation.

Section 2.2: Stylistic Comparisons with Competitors

The 1957 Chevrolet Bel Air didn't exist in a vacuum; it was born into a highly competitive automotive landscape where styling had become a primary battleground among American manufacturers. A comprehensive understanding of Bel Air's design significance requires examining how it compares to its contemporary rivals, particularly from Ford and Chrysler.

Ford's offerings for 1957 represented a significant departure from previous designs. The Ford Fairlane, which competed directly with the Bel Air, featured a longer, lower profile with a distinctive side scallop and modest tailfins. Ford had embraced what they called their "Lifeguard Design" philosophy, emphasizing horizontal lines and a certain squareness that contrasted with Chevrolet's more curvaceous approach. Ford's design language incorporated a wide, horizontal grille and dual headlights on higher trims, clearly responding to the industry trend toward more elaborate front-end treatments. While handsome and modern, Ford's styling was arguably more conservative and less flamboyant than the Bel Air's dramatic presentation.

Chrysler Corporation, under the design leadership of Virgil Exner, had begun what they termed the "Forward Look" in 1955, which reached full expression by 1957. Chrysler's high-end models, notably

15

the Plymouth Fury, Dodge Royal, and Chrysler 300C, featured dramatic styling with soaring tailfins, extensive use of chrome, and a distinctive forward-thrusting stance. These vehicles embraced excess as virtue, with some models sporting fins that extended well beyond the rear deck and chrome applications that bordered on the theatrical. Chrysler positioned their vehicles as the pinnacle of jet-age styling, aiming to capture consumers who wanted the most visually striking automobiles on the road.

Against these competitors, Chevrolet differentiated the Bel Air through a carefully calibrated blend of boldness and restraint. While the '57 Bel Air certainly embraced the tailfin phenomenon, it did so with more restraint than Chrysler's dramatic interpretations. The Bel Air's fins were integrated more naturally into the body lines, rising organically from the quarter panels rather than appearing as separate design elements grafted onto the car. This gave the Bel Air a sense of wholeness in its design that some competitors lacked.

Furthermore, Chevrolet distinguished the Bel Air through its unique application of chrome and color. While Ford tended toward more restrained brightwork and Chrysler often applied chrome with abandon, the Bel Air struck a middle ground with strategic chrome placement that highlighted the car's natural lines rather than overwhelming them. The anodized aluminum side panel, available in contrasting colors, was utterly unique in the industry and gave the Bel Air an instantly recognizable signature element.

Perhaps most importantly, Chevrolet positioned the Bel Air as attainable luxury, offering high-style design at a price point significantly below that of comparable Chrysler products, while providing more visual flair than Ford's offerings. This value proposition was reflected in the design itself; the Bel Air looked more expensive than it was, borrowing design cues from higher-end vehicles but executing them at a price point accessible to middle-class Americans.

By analyzing the competitive landscape, we can see that Bel Air's most remarkable achievement was finding the visual sweet spot in American automotive design: elaborate enough to capture the imagination of style-conscious consumers, yet restrained enough to avoid the excesses that would make some of its competitors look dated within a few years. This balance helps explain why the '57 Bel Air has endured as an icon while many of its contemporaries have faded into mere historical curiosities.

Section 2.3: How Chevrolet Differentiated the Bel Air

The 1957 Chevrolet Bel Air emerged as a distinct personality in the automotive landscape through deliberate design choices that set it apart from both its corporate cousins and industry competitors. Chevrolet positioned the Bel Air as the perfect balance between luxury and accessibility, more refined than Ford's offerings but more attainable than Chrysler's premium models.

The most successful differentiation strategy employed by Chevrolet was the Bel Air's visual presence. While competitors like Ford emphasized horizontal lines and substantial bulk, Chevrolet created a lighter, more graceful silhouette. The Bel Air appeared to float above the road, with an airy greenhouse and delicate pillars, contrasting with Ford's more substantial, planted appearance. The Bel Air's distinctive side complemented this visual lightness, with a trim, sweeping spear that suggested motion even when the car was parked.

Chevrolet also differentiated the Bel Air through its detailed ornamentation. Unlike Chrysler's sometimes overwrought decoration or Ford's more restrained approach, the Bel Air featured precisely placed chrome elements that enhanced its lines without overwhelming them. The gold anodized grille emblem and hood ornament gave the Bel Air an air of sophistication that belied its middle-market positioning.

Color played another crucial role in the Bel Air's distinct identity. While competitors offered two-tone paint schemes, none matched the variety and vibrancy of Chevrolet's palette. The company's marketing materials highlighted these exclusive color combinations, effectively turning the paint options into status symbols themselves. This approach made the Bel Air instantly recognizable on American roads, a critical advantage in the increasingly competitive market.

Perhaps most importantly, Chevrolet managed to imbue the Bel Air with a sense of accessible luxury. It wasn't trying to be the most luxurious car on the market; that territory belonged to Cadillac and Imperial. Instead, the Bel Air represented attainable elegance, offering features and styling cues previously reserved for more expensive vehicles. The dashboard design, with its aircraft-inspired instrument cluster, exemplified this approach: sophisticated yet not intimidating.

Chevrolet's marketing reinforced this differentiation, positioning the Bel Air as "The Hot One" and emphasizing its combination of style, performance, and value. This careful market positioning elevated the Bel Air above its competitors and even other Chevrolet models, establishing it as an aspirational yet attainable American dream on wheels. This distinction continues to resonate with enthusiasts to this day.

Section 2.4: Color and Finish Innovations

The 1957 Chevrolet Bel Air didn't just redefine automotive proportions and styling; it revolutionized how Americans thought about car colors and finishes. In an era when automotive design was increasingly reflecting America's optimistic post-war sensibilities,

Chevrolet's approach to color and chrome on the '57 Bel Air represented both artistic expression and technical innovation.

The Revolutionary Color Palette

The 1957 Bel Air's color palette stands as one of its most memorable and defining characteristics. Chevrolet offered an unprecedented range of vibrant colors that captured the exuberant mood of 1950s America, from Tropical Turquoise to Matador Red, from Colonial Cream to Larkspur Blue. Each hue was carefully developed to complement the car's flowing lines and chrome accents.

What truly set the '57 Bel Air apart was its sophisticated use of two-tone combinations. These weren't merely aesthetic choices but strategic design elements that accentuated the car's distinctive body lines. The most iconic combinations featured a roof in one color with the body in another, often separated by the sweeping chrome trim that flowed along the car's flanks. This design approach visually elongated the vehicle while creating a sense of movement even when parked.

The two-tone arrangements weren't arbitrary; they represented a carefully orchestrated visual harmony. Designers paired colors to create either subtle, elegant contrasts or bold, eye-catching statements. The India Ivory roof over Tropical Turquoise, for example, became an instantly recognizable combination that embodied the car's cheerful confidence.

The significance of these color choices extended beyond mere decoration. They reflected broader cultural trends toward optimism, expressiveness, and personal preference in the booming post-war economy. Offering buyers this palette of colors and combinations was a marketing masterstroke that allowed customers to express their individual taste while maintaining the Bel Air's cohesive design identity.

Behind these vibrant hues lie significant advancements in paint technology. Chevrolet implemented new acrylic lacquer paints that offered deeper, more lustrous finishes with improved durability compared to earlier automotive paints. These technical improvements allowed colors to shine more brilliantly in sunlight and resist fading far better than their predecessors. The paint processes themselves were refined to ensure more consistent application across the vast production numbers, maintaining quality standards that contributed to Bel Air's reputation for excellence.

Chrome Applications

Chrome defined the aesthetic of 1950s American automobiles, and nowhere was this more evident than on the '57 Bel Air. Chevrolet's liberal yet tasteful application of chrome elevated the car from a means of transportation to a rolling sculpture.

The manufacturing techniques behind the Bel Air's chrome elements represented the pinnacle of mid-century industrial processes. Chevrolet refined its electroplating methods to ensure exceptional brightness and durability. Each chrome component underwent multiple plating steps: first copper, then nickel, and finally chromium. This layered approach yielded a deep, reflective finish that resisted pitting and corrosion more effectively than previous techniques.

The engineering challenges were considerable. Maintaining consistent plating thickness across complex shapes required precise control of electrical current and chemical composition in the plating baths. Significant components, such as bumpers, required massive plating tanks and specialized handling equipment. Despite these challenges, Chevrolet achieved remarkable consistency across the hundreds of thousands of vehicles produced.

What distinguished the '57 Bel Air's chrome work wasn't just its quality but its strategic placement for maximum visual impact. The front grille, with its distinctive horizontal bar design, created a face that was both friendly and imposing. The massive front and rear bumpers, with their integrated guards and extensions, bookended the design with bold statements of solidity and luxury.

Perhaps most ingeniously, Chevrolet designers used chrome as a visual tool to accentuate the car's lines. The sweeping side spear, which began at the headlights and flowed back to form the tailfin outline, became a signature element, creating a visual dividing line for two-tone paint schemes while suggesting forward motion. Additional trim pieces adorned the hood, trunk, and window surrounds, while Bel Air-specific emblems and script badges announced the model's premium status.

These chrome elements weren't merely decorative additions; they were integral to the car's design language, highlighting architectural features and creating visual rhythm. Their placement drew the eye along the car's contours, emphasizing its length, width, and the graceful transition between different volumes of the body.

Together, the revolutionary color palette and masterful chrome applications transformed the 1957 Bel Air into more than just a means of transportation. They created an object of beauty and desire that reflected the confidence and prosperity of mid-century America, a gleaming, colorful expression of automotive optimism that continues to captivate enthusiasts more than six decades later.

The Revolutionary Rear Treatment

The 1957 Bel Air's rear styling stands as its most distinctive and influential design element, representing the pinnacle of America's fascination with aeronautical influences in automotive design. Chevrolet's stylists created a rear treatment that was both dramatic and refined, establishing a visual signature that would become instantly recognizable on highways across America.

1957 Chevrolet Bel Air: Cruising Through Time

The development of the Bel Air's distinctive tailfins was the culmination of a design trend that had been building throughout the 1950s. Unlike the more extreme fins found on contemporary Cadillacs or Chryslers, the Bel Air's fins struck a perfect balance, prominent enough to make a statement yet integrated harmoniously with the overall body design. These tailfins weren't merely decorative; they extended naturally from the rear quarter panels in a sweeping upward motion that enhanced the car's sense of forward momentum even when parked.

Harley Earl and his design team drew inspiration from the aviation industry, particularly from the sleek profiles of contemporary jet aircraft. The fins were carefully sculpted to appear substantial without overwhelming the car's proportions, tapering elegantly toward their peaks. This attention to detail gave the Bel Air a sophisticated presence that distinguished it from competitors who often employed more exaggerated fin treatments.

The tail light design and placement represented another triumph of the '57 Bel Air's rear styling. Chevrolet abandoned the more conventional horizontal taillights of the previous models in favor of vertically oriented units integrated into the tailfins. These distinctive bullet-shaped lamps appeared to float within the fin structure, creating a visual highlight that drew attention to the fins' graceful contours. The tail lights featured a unique lens pattern that produced a distinctive illumination pattern at night, making the Bel Air instantly identifiable even from a distance.

The relationship between the taillights and the rear chrome bumper was meticulously orchestrated. The bumper's design incorporated cutouts that framed the reverse lights and license plate, creating a sophisticated three-dimensional effect that added depth to the rear view. Chrome trim pieces traced the edges of the fins, catching sunlight and emphasizing their sculptural quality without appearing excessive or gaudy.

Perhaps most remarkably, the Bel Air's rear design looked both futuristic and timeless. While clearly a product of its era, the restraint shown by Chevrolet's designers gave the car a lasting appeal that would help establish it as an enduring icon of American automotive design. The Revolutionary Rear Treatment of the '57 Bel Air didn't just complement the car's overall design; it elevated it, becoming the exclamation point on what many consider Detroit's masterpiece.

Section 2.5: The Design Team Behind the Legend

Behind the iconic silhouette and revolutionary styling of the 1957 Chevrolet Bel Air stood a remarkable team of visionaries, engineers, and artists who collectively created one of Detroit's most enduring masterpieces. While Harley Earl's influence loomed large over GM's design direction, the 1957 Bel Air was a genuinely collaborative achievement that required countless hours of dedication from a diverse group of talented professionals.

At the helm of Chevrolet's design efforts was Clare MacKichan, the Chief Designer who oversaw the evolution of the Tri-Five Chevrolets. MacKichan's ability to translate Earl's broader vision into practical yet beautiful designs was instrumental in the Bel Air. Working closely with Earl, MacKichan pushed for the distinctive tailfins and chrome applications that would become hallmarks of the '57 model.

The studio team included several unsung heroes whose contributions were vital. Carl Renner, a gifted stylist who had worked on previous Chevrolet models, was particularly influential in developing the Bel Air's side profile and its distinctive side trim, creating the perfect canvas for the two-tone color applications. Chuck Jordan, who would later rise to prominence as GM's Vice President of Design, contributed significantly to the front-end styling that gave the Bel Air its confident face.

On the engineering side, Ed Cole served as Chevrolet's chief engineer during this period. Cole's mechanical genius complemented the stylists' artistic vision, ensuring that equally impressive mechanical components matched the beautiful exterior. His team confronted numerous challenges in maintaining the car's sleek proportions while accommodating necessary mechanical systems and ensuring structural integrity.

The '57 Bel Air also benefited from executive champions who protected the design's integrity through the development process. Notably, Chevrolet General Manager Thomas Keating provided crucial support when manufacturing concerns threatened to dilute some of the car's most distinctive styling elements. When production engineers expressed concerns about the complex curve of the rear fenders and tailfin assembly, Keating backed the design team, insisting that solutions be found rather than compromises made.

These designers and engineers faced significant technical limitations that required innovative thinking. The sweeping windshield and wraparound rear glass presented manufacturing challenges that required new approaches to glass forming and installation. The intricate grille design demanded precision die-casting techniques that pushed the boundaries of the era's manufacturing capabilities.

The most significant challenge arose from manufacturing constraints related to the car's extensive use of chrome and complex body stampings. The design team worked closely with production engineers to develop new stamping processes that could achieve the deep body-side sculpturing while maintaining consistent quality. Similarly, the application of chrome trim required new fixture designs and assembly techniques to ensure proper fit and finish.

The success of the '57 Bel Air stands as a testament to this team's ability to overcome these obstacles. Their collective expertise, creativity, and determination transformed what might have been just another annual model update into an enduring icon of American automotive design. While Harley Earl's design philosophy provided the North Star that guided their efforts, it was this dedicated team of professionals who navigated the complex journey from concept to production, creating in the process not just a car but a lasting cultural symbol.

Section 2.6: From Drawing Board to Production Reality

The journey from concept sketch to showroom floor for the 1957 Bel Air represented one of General Motors' most ambitious production undertakings of the era. This transformation required not only artistic vision but also engineering precision and manufacturing innovation on an unprecedented scale.

Executive Reviews and Sign-offs

The path to production for the '57 Bel Air involved a rigorous series of executive reviews that began nearly three years before the model's introduction. Harley Earl's design studio first presented conceptual renderings to Chevrolet's executive committee in late 1954, which sparked initial approval and led to the development of small-scale models.

By early 1955, as the '55 models were rolling into showrooms, full-sized clay models of the proposed '57 design were already being scrutinized by GM's senior leadership. These review sessions were notoriously demanding, with Ed Cole, Chevrolet's general manager at the time, often requesting multiple revisions to ensure the design struck a balance between aesthetic appeal and manufacturing practicality.

The final approval came in stages, with the basic body shape receiving the go-ahead in mid-1955, followed by incremental approvals for exterior trim elements, interior configurations, and color schemes. Each approval milestone required sign-off from multiple divisions, including design, engineering, manufacturing, and marketing, creating a complex web of decision-making that had to remain coordinated despite occasional interdepartmental tensions.

Consumer Testing and Focus Groups

In a practice somewhat ahead of its time, Chevrolet conducted limited consumer testing for the '57 Bel Air design. While not as sophisticated as modern focus groups, these sessions brought potential customers to viewing rooms where they could react to the new design elements under consideration.

Notably, the tailfin design underwent several revisions based on consumer feedback, particularly in the testing phase. Initially, some executives worried the fins might be too dramatic for Chevrolet's middle-market positioning, but consumer reactions strongly favored the bold styling choice.

The dashboard layout also benefited from consumer input, with early testers helping refine the placement of controls and the visibility of instruments. These sessions revealed a strong positive response to the aircraft-inspired dashboard elements, reinforcing the design team's instinct to incorporate jet-age aesthetics throughout the vehicle.

Section 2.7: Production Engineering Solutions

Tooling and Manufacturing Innovations

Bringing the '57 Bel Air's complex shapes to production required significant innovations in tooling and manufacturing. The sweeping curves and tight tolerances of the body panels demanded new approaches to die-making and stamping operations.

The most significant challenge came from the compound curves in the rear quarter panels, which housed the tailfins. Traditional stamping methods struggled to form these complex shapes without thinning or tearing the sheet metal. Engineers developed a multi-stage stamping process that progressively formed the metal, allowing for the dramatic contours while maintaining structural integrity.

The two-tone paint schemes, particularly on the Bel Air Sport Coupe, necessitated precision masking techniques that had to be integrated into the production line workflow. New jigs and fixtures were specifically designed to ensure the consistent application of color breaks across thousands of vehicles.

Chrome application represented another production hurdle. The Bel Air's extensive brightwork required innovations in both the plating process and the fixtures used to hold components during the dipping process. A new quality control system was implemented specifically to monitor the finish quality of chrome components, as any imperfection would be immediately noticeable against the Bel Air's gleaming paintwork.

Quality Control Processes

The ambitious design of the '57 Bel Air demanded equally ambitious quality control measures. Chevrolet implemented a multi-stage inspection process that began with component-level checks and continued through final assembly.

Body panels were subjected to light tunnels, where inspectors could detect even minor surface imperfections before the painting process. After paint application, similar inspections ensured color consistency and finish quality. The final assembly inspection was particularly rigorous for Bel Air models, with dedicated inspectors checking trim alignment, panel gaps, and functional aspects of all luxury features.

Perhaps most telling was the implementation of a customer perspective inspection, where randomly selected completed vehicles were evaluated as a consumer would experience them, from visual appeal at a distance to the feel of interior controls and the sound of the door closing. This holistic approach to quality control helped ensure that the production reality lived up to the original vision of the design studio.

Through this multifaceted process of approval, engineering, and quality control, Chevrolet successfully transformed the ambitious '57 Bel Air design from artistic concept to production reality, creating a vehicle that would become not just a sales success but an enduring cultural icon.

Chapter 3: Tailfins and Chrome: Jet Age Aesthetics and Styling Innovations

Section 3.1: Chrome as Art, Defining the 1957 Bel Air's Elegance and Innovation

The 1957 Chevrolet Bel Air's masterful use of chrome transcended mere decoration, becoming a fundamental design language that communicated the vehicle's status and technological aspirations. Chrome elements were strategically placed to accentuate the car's most distinctive features and create visual pathways that guided the eye across its sculpted form.

The front end featured a bold chrome grille composed of horizontal bars that emphasized the car's width, creating an impression of solidity and presence on the road. This grille was framed by chrome-surrounded headlights, which themselves were punctuated by subtle chrome eyebrows that added a touch of sophistication. The massive front bumper, with its prominent chrome guards and center extension, served not only a protective function but also anchored the visual weight of the front fascia.

Along the body sides, chrome moldings performed multiple visual tasks. The spear-like side trim divided the two-tone paint schemes while simultaneously creating a visual impression of forward motion even when the car was stationary. These strips weren't merely affixed to flat surfaces; they followed and emphasized the subtle body contours, highlighting the car's curves and enhancing its three-dimensional presence. The window surrounds, fully encased in chrome, created a cohesive visual frame for the greenhouse area, adding perceived value while drawing attention to the airy, expansive cabin.

Perhaps most distinctive was how chrome was deployed at the rear, where it outlined and accentuated the now-iconic tailfins. Chrome strips traced the upper edge of each fin, while additional brightwork surrounded the distinctive taillights. The rear bumper, substantial in its own right, featured integrated exhaust ports that suggested jet propulsion, reinforcing the aerospace aesthetic that defined the era.

Each chrome element served as a visual cue, communicating the Bel Air's position at the pinnacle of Chevrolet's lineup. The thoughtful placement created hierarchy and rhythm across the car's surfaces, transforming what could have been visual excess into a coherent design statement that spoke to America's mid-century optimism and technical prowess.

Section 3.2: The Gleam of Greatness, Chrome as the Soul of the 1957 Bel Air

The 1957 Chevrolet Bel Air's magnificent chrome treatment wasn't merely decorative; it was a carefully orchestrated design language that communicated status, technological advancement, and the exuberance of the Jet Age. The strategic placement of chrome elements throughout the vehicle served both aesthetic and functional purposes, transforming the Bel Air into a rolling sculpture that captured America's optimistic spirit.

Chrome adorned the Bel Air at critical visual focal points, beginning with the bold front grille that announced the car's presence. The massive horizontal grille bar, flanked by the distinctive dual headlights, created an impression of width and stability. This expansive chrome treatment visually anchored the vehicle while drawing the eye across its impressive stance. The bumper's substantial chrome treatment reinforced this effect, providing both visual protection and safety assurance.

Along the Bel Air's flanks, chrome side spears served multiple design functions. These polished strips visually lengthened the profile while simultaneously breaking up the expansive sheet metal, preventing the larger body panels from appearing too heavy or monolithic. On Bel Air models, these side spears incorporated distinctive anodized aluminum inserts with a gold anodized finish, creating a sophisticated two-tone effect that distinguished the premium model from its more modest stablemates.

The relationship between the chrome elements and the car's painted surfaces was carefully calculated. Chrome acted as a framing device, highlighting body contours and accentuating the dramatic tailfins. Around windows, chrome trim (known as "bright metal moldings" in GM parlance) served to visually lighten the greenhouse while providing a finished, premium appearance to these transition areas.

Perhaps most emblematic of the Bel Air's chrome philosophy was the dramatic rear treatment. Chrome encircled the distinctive dual tail lights, creating what designers called "artillery shells" that echoed jet engine imagery. The rear bumper incorporated dramatic chrome exhaust ports, reinforcing the jet-inspired design language. The iconic Chevrolet script and Bel Air emblems, themselves chrome masterpieces, provided brand identification while functioning as jewelry-like accents.

Interior chrome elements maintained this design dialogue, with chrome instrument bezels, control knobs, shift indicators, and trim pieces creating points of visual interest and tactile luxury. These gleaming touchpoints reminded occupants of the car's premium status every time they interacted with the vehicle.

Beyond mere decoration, the Bel Air's chrome treatment served to emphasize the car's underlying structure, highlighting door seams, outlining windows, and accentuating the hood and trunk openings. This integration of functional areas into the aesthetic design demonstrated GM's sophisticated approach to styling during this golden era of American automotive design, where chrome wasn't simply applied as an afterthought but was fundamentally integrated into the vehicle's visual identity.

Section 3.3: Chrome Dreams: Chevrolet's 1957 Bel Air and the Art of Aspirational Marketing

Chevrolet's marketing strategy for the 1957 Bel Air masterfully capitalized on America's fascination with chrome, creating what industry insiders referred to as the "chrome dream" approach to automobile promotion. This strategy positioned Chrome not merely as decoration, but as a signifier of luxury, modernity, and technological advancement. In advertisements spanning magazines, television, and billboards, Chevrolet consistently highlighted the Bel Air's gleaming chrome elements, often using dramatic lighting to create dazzling reflections that captured the viewer's attention.

The marketing language itself employed evocative terminology, with copywriters describing the chrome as "jewel-like," "gleaming with distinction," and offering "brilliant personality." One particularly successful campaign referred to the Bel Air as "The Hot One with the

1957 Chevrolet Bel Air: Cruising Through Time

Cool Chrome," cleverly connecting the car's performance capabilities with its styling elements. Dealership promotional materials instructed salespeople to draw specific attention to chrome features, suggesting they invite customers to run their fingers along the trim to appreciate both its visual appeal and tangible quality.

Perhaps most effectively, Chevrolet's advertisements placed the chrome-laden Bel Air in distinctly upscale environments, outside exclusive restaurants, country clubs, and modern architectural marvels, visually associating the relatively affordable Chevrolet with a luxury lifestyle previously reserved for more expensive automobiles. This aspirational positioning was revolutionary, suggesting that middle-class Americans could access sophistication and style through the ownership of Chevrolet.

The "chrome dream" approach extended beyond visual imagery into the realm of consumer psychology. Marketing materials emphasized how neighbors would admire the Bel Air's gleaming presence in one's driveway, suggesting that the chrome elements served as visual shorthand for the owner's good taste and success. Period sales brochures featured fold-out panoramic images specifically designed to showcase the continuous chrome body side moldings, often printed with metallic inks to simulate the reflective quality of the actual trim.

This marketing approach proved remarkably effective, creating insatiable consumer demand and establishing chrome as the definitive design element of the era. More importantly, it cemented in the American consciousness an association between the '57 Bel Air and an optimistic, prosperous vision of mid-century life. This association has endured long after the chrome dream faded from other contemporaneous vehicles.

Section 3.4: Color and Trim Innovations

The 1957 Chevrolet Bel Air represented one of the most ambitious deployments of color in American automotive history, utilizing color not merely as decoration but as a fundamental element of the vehicle's design identity. This approach to color and trim would help define an era and cement Bel Air's place as a cultural icon.

A. The expanded color palette: standard and special order options

The 1957 Bel Air's color palette represented a dramatic departure from the more conservative options of previous decades. Chevrolet offered customers an impressive 17 solid colors and 15 two-tone combinations, a range unprecedented in the company's history. Standard colors included vibrant options like Tropical Turquoise, Matador Red, and Harbor Blue, while more subtle choices like Onyx Black and Adobe Beige catered to conservative buyers.

Chevrolet also introduced a series of special-order colors for customers seeking exclusivity. These included Corvette-derived hues like Aztec Copper and Imperial Ivory, available at additional cost but providing discerning buyers with truly distinctive options. Dealerships maintained color chips and full-color brochures showing all combinations, allowing customers to visualize their selections before ordering. The expanded palette reflected Chevrolet's understanding that color had become a critical factor in purchase decisions, particularly among younger buyers and those influenced by contemporary home design trends that similarly embraced vibrant colors.

B. Two-tone and three-tone paint schemes

The most striking aspect of the Bel Air's color approach was its sophisticated use of multiple colors on a single vehicle. Two-tone schemes were carefully designed to accentuate the car's dramatic lines, with secondary colors typically applied to the roof and sometimes extending down to the vehicle's beltline or rear quarters. Popular combinations included Larkspur Blue with India Ivory, and Matador Red with Arctic White, each creating a visual impact impossible with single-color applications.

The most distinctive Bel Airs featured three-tone color schemes, representing the pinnacle of mid-century automotive color design. These arrangements typically featured a primary body color, a contrasting roof color, and a third accent color applied to the side coves or inserts between the chrome trim on the rear quarters. The three-tone approach transformed the vehicle into a rolling color composition that highlighted its sculptural qualities from every angle. These elaborate paint schemes required specialized masking techniques at the factory and contributed significantly to the car's production costs, but the visual impact justified the additional expense.

C. Interior color coordination and materials

Chevrolet's designers paid equal attention to the Bel Air's interior, developing sophisticated color coordination between exterior and interior components. Upholstery fabrics were explicitly designed for the model year, featuring distinctive patterns that complemented the vehicle's jet-age aesthetic. The standard interior featured color-keyed vinyl and patterned cloth combinations, with premium Bel Air models offering more elaborate treatments including textured inserts and contrasting piping.

Interior color schemes were carefully calibrated to harmonize with exterior colors. A Tropical Turquoise exterior might be paired with a turquoise and gray interior featuring silver-flecked fabric, creating a cohesive design statement inside and out. Dashboard components were color-matched to the exterior, often incorporating two colors, with the lower portion of the dash matching the primary body color.

Even details, such as steering wheels, featured color-coordinated elements, demonstrating Chevrolet's comprehensive approach to color design. The materials themselves represented significant innovations, with new vinyl formulations offering improved durability and resistance to fading, addressing complaints from previous model years.

D. Special edition color packages and regional variations

Beyond the standard offerings, Chevrolet introduced several special edition color packages for the 1957 Bel Air, often tied to specific promotional campaigns or regional preferences. The "Spring Special" package, launched in April 1957, featured exclusive Sierra Gold and Adobe Beige two-tone combinations with matching interiors. In southern states, Chevrolet offered the "Sunshine Special" with tropical-inspired color schemes, including Coronado Yellow with Tropical Turquoise accents.

Regional variations were particularly notable, with certain color combinations proving popular in specific markets. California dealers reported strong demand for brighter combinations, while Northeastern markets favored more subdued schemes. Some regional dealership networks created their own special editions to cater to local tastes - notably the "Mountain Laurel" special in the Pacific Northwest, featuring a unique Highland Green with a silver roof treatment not available in standard Chevrolet literature.

The manufacturer also accommodated fleet customers with custom color programs. Police departments could order Bel Airs in departmental colors, while taxi companies had access to high-visibility color schemes with special-wear interior materials. This flexibility in color offerings demonstrated Chevrolet's commitment to using color as both a marketing tool and a means of product differentiation in an increasingly competitive market, establishing practices that continue in automotive marketing to this day.

Section 3.5: The Critical Details

The 1957 Chevrolet Bel Air's enduring appeal lies not just in its overall silhouette but in the meticulous attention to detail that distinguished it from competitors and even its predecessors. These critical design elements combined to create a cohesive visual statement that remains instantly recognizable decades later. The iconic front grille of the '57 Bel Air represented a significant evolution from previous Chevrolet designs.

Moving away from the horizontal emphasis of the 1955-56 models, the '57 introduced a wider, lower grille with an intricate egg-crate pattern that stretched across the full width of the car. Chrome-surrounded rectangular openings created a sophisticated mesh appearance, simultaneously conveying luxury and sportiness. The grille was integrated seamlessly with the front bumper assembly, creating a unified face for the vehicle that projected both elegance and a hint of aggression. This grille design became so distinctive that it has often been replicated on custom cars and even influenced modern Chevrolet concept vehicles.

Headlight and taillight styling on the '57 Bel Air showcased GM's innovative approach to functional elements as design features. The headlights featured chrome bezels with a subtle hooded effect, giving the front end a slightly furrowed, purposeful expression. These were complemented by the parking lights, which were incorporated into the mesh grille rather than being separate units. At the rear, the taillights were even more revolutionary.

Designed to echo jet exhaust outlets, these round lenses were housed in chrome nacelles that protruded slightly from the tailfins. When illuminated at night, they created a distinctive pattern that made the Bel Air unmistakable even from a distance. This integration of lighting elements as styling features represented a significant departure from the more utilitarian approach of earlier automotive designs.

Hood ornaments and emblems on the '57 Bel Air served as jewelry for the vehicle, carefully designed to enhance its premium position. The hood featured Chevrolet's iconic "jet bird" ornament, a stylized forward-leaning bird that embodied motion even when the car was stationary. This chrome sculpture caught the sunlight dramatically, leading the eye backward along the hood's centerline.

The Bel Air's identity was further reinforced through the strategic placement of nameplates and Chevrolet bowties on the hood, trunk, and front fenders. The Bel Air models featured additional gold-accented trim that distinguished them from lower-tier Chevrolet models, with script lettering on the rear quarters and special crossed-flag emblems denoting V8-equipped cars. These emblems weren't merely badges but integrated design elements that contributed to the car's premium character.

The wheel covers and styling options offered for the '57 Bel Air reflected the era's fascination with space-age design. Standard full wheel covers featured a complex starburst pattern with simulated knock-off spinners in the center, reminiscent of racing wheels but executed with a more luxurious flair. Optional wire wheel covers, often referred to as "spinners," added a touch of extra sophistication.

The relationship between the wheels and the body was carefully considered, with the wheel openings sculpted to complement the car's flowing lines. White sidewall tires were popular options that further enhanced the car's visual appeal, creating a crisp contrast with the colorful bodies and chrome wheel covers. These wheel treatments provided the finishing touch to the Bel Air's ground-hugging stance, visually anchoring the flamboyant body design while adding their own distinctive character.

Together, these critical details transformed what could have been merely a handsome car into an automotive icon. The '57 Bel Air's enduring popularity can be attributed to how these elements work in concert, creating a harmonious design that remains fresh and compelling more than six decades after it first appeared in Chevrolet showrooms.

Section 3.6: Interior Design Elements

The interior of the 1957 Chevrolet Bel Air represented as much of a design revolution as its exterior, creating a cohesive aesthetic experience that extended the Jet Age theme throughout the vehicle. Stepping inside a '57 Bel Air was meant to evoke the same sense of modern luxury and forward-thinking optimism that defined the exterior styling.

The dashboard layout and instrument panel of the Bel Air broke new ground with its aircraft-inspired design. The horizontal speedometer, dubbed the "Sweep-Sight" panel, featured a distinctive curved design that enhanced visibility while evoking the look of an airplane's instrument cluster. Chrome bezels framed each gauge, complementing the exterior brightwork and creating a sense of continuity. The dashboard itself abandoned the heavy, bulky look of previous generations in favor of a sleeker, more streamlined appearance with integrated controls that float within the panel rather than being merely attached to it.

Seating designs in the '57 Bel Air represented a significant leap forward in both style and comfort. The premium Bel Air trim offered a range of upholstery options, with the most distinctive being the tri-tone pattern that featured textured cloth inserts and vinyl bolsters. These patterns often coordinated with exterior color schemes, creating a thoughtfully designed environment. The bench seats featured a lower profile than previous models, enhancing the car's spacious feel while providing improved support. For buyers seeking ultimate luxury, leather upholstery was available as a special-order option, often in bright color combinations that would seem audacious by today's more conservative standards.

Luxury touches abounded throughout the Bel Air's interior. Chrome accents appeared on door handles, window cranks, and control knobs, creating bright points of interest throughout the cabin. The steering wheel featured a unique design with a full horn ring and a transparent top section, which improved visibility of the instruments. Armrests were generously padded, and door panels featured sculpted designs that mirrored the flowing lines of the exterior. The optional tissue dispenser and cigarette lighter spoke to the era's definition of convenience and luxury. At the same time, the available "Autronic Eye" automatic headlight dimmer represented cutting-edge technology that enhanced the car's futuristic appeal.

Perhaps most remarkable about the Bel Air's interior design was its seamless relationship with exterior themes. The dashboard's horizontal emphasis echoed the car's wide, low stance, while interior color schemes were carefully coordinated with exterior paint options. The Bel Air's renowned two-tone and tri-tone exterior paint schemes often continued inside, with door panels and seats featuring complementary color combinations. Even the pattern of the upholstery suggested movement and speed, with diagonal lines and geometric shapes that reflected the dynamism of the exterior styling.

The radiused corners and soft curves found throughout the interior space created a sense of continuity with the exterior's aerodynamic profile. This integration of interior and exterior design elements represented a sophisticated approach to automotive design that was relatively uncommon for mass-market vehicles of the era. Rather than treating the interior as merely functional, Chevrolet designers recognized the importance of creating a holistic experience that began with the car's striking exterior and continued seamlessly once the driver and passengers were inside.

This thoughtful integration of design themes helped establish the 1957 Bel Air as not merely a stylish automobile but as a complete design statement, one that continues to influence how we think about automotive interiors and their relationship to exterior styling more than six decades later.

Section 3.7: Design Team and Process

The iconic 1957 Chevrolet Bel Air was not simply the product of automotive manufacturing but rather the culmination of artistic vision, engineering prowess, and corporate strategy. Behind this legendary vehicle stood a talented team of designers working within General Motors' sophisticated styling infrastructure.

Leading GM's styling department was the legendary Harley Earl, whose influence on American automotive design is truly unparalleled. Earl, who had established GM's Art and Color Section in 1927 (later renamed the Styling Section), pioneered the concept that cars should be sold on both appearance and mechanical performance. By the mid-1950s, Earl had firmly established GM as a design leader in the industry, and his personal aesthetic preferences for long, low proportions and aircraft-inspired elements directly influenced the development of the '57 Bel Air.

Under Earl's direction, the Chevrolet studio was led by Clare MacKichan, who oversaw the design evolution that culminated in the '57 model. MacKichan worked with a team that included stylists Carl Renner and Chuck Jordan, whose contributions to the distinctive fins and chrome details became defining elements of the car. Renner, in particular, is often credited with developing some of the most unique styling cues that made the '57 Bel Air instantly recognizable.

The design process began nearly three years before production, with preliminary sketches exploring various styling directions. These early concepts underwent rigorous review in design meetings where

Earl would often make decisive, sometimes dramatic changes to the proposals. The iterative process continued through clay modeling stages, where three-dimensional forms allowed designers to refine the vehicle's proportions and surface treatments.

Within General Motors' corporate structure, an internal design competition fostered creativity and excellence. Different divisions, including Chevrolet, Buick, Oldsmobile, Pontiac, and Cadillac, competed for approval and resources, with each studio striving to create the most compelling designs. This competitive environment prompted the Chevrolet team to develop distinctive styling that would not only stand out against external competitors but also within GM's own lineup.

The journey from concept to production involved transitioning from free-form artistic sketches to increasingly precise engineering specifications. The clay models eventually gave way to production prototypes where manufacturing constraints had to be reconciled with design aspirations. The distinctive tailfins, for instance, required careful engineering to ensure they could be manufactured adequately while maintaining their dramatic visual impact.

Earl's famous "longer, lower, wider" philosophy reached its zenith during this period, and the Bel Air represented this vision perfectly. The design team successfully balanced Earl's preference for dramatic styling with Chevrolet's position as GM's affordable, mass-market division, creating a vehicle that offered visual excitement without the price tag of its Buick or Cadillac cousins.

By the time the clay model was approved for production, countless hours of refinement had transformed the initial concept into a cohesive, market-ready design. Engineering teams then collaborated closely with the stylists to ensure that mechanical components could be integrated without compromising the car's visual appeal.

1957 Chevrolet Bel Air: Cruising Through Time

The success of the '57 Bel Air's design process is evident not only in its initial market reception but also in its enduring status as a design icon. The seamless collaboration between Harley Earl's styling leadership, the talented Chevrolet studio designers, and GM's engineering teams created more than just another annual model; they produced automotive art that continues to captivate enthusiasts decades later.

Chapter 4: Under the Hood: Powertrains, Engineering, and Technical Specifications

Section 4.1: Chassis and Suspension Developments

The 1957 Chevrolet Bel Air represented a significant advancement in chassis and suspension technology, combining robust engineering with innovative design to create a platform that would become legendary for both its durability and adaptability.

At the foundation of Bel Air's mechanical excellence was its frame architecture. Chevrolet engineers employed a sturdy X-frame design that departed significantly from the perimeter frames used by many competitors. This X-configuration provided exceptional rigidity while maintaining relatively light weight, creating a solid foundation that contributed to the car's reputation for durability. The frame utilized box-section side rails with strategic reinforcements at high-stress points, providing a stable platform that resisted flexing even under demanding driving conditions.

1957 Chevrolet Bel Air: Cruising Through Time

The front suspension system featured one of the period's most significant innovations: the ball-joint design. This represented a major evolution from the kingpin setups used in earlier models and by many competitors. The ball-joint configuration allowed for more precise wheel control while reducing maintenance requirements. The upper and lower control arms worked in concert with coil springs to provide a remarkable balance between comfort and handling for the era. This system also incorporated a stabilizer bar (also known as an anti-roll bar) on higher-performance models, further enhancing cornering capabilities.

In the rear, Chevrolet maintained a semi-elliptical leaf spring suspension, but made significant refinements over previous iterations. The 1957 model featured longer, more progressively rated leaf springs that provided better articulation and load distribution. The four-link attachment method, featuring front and rear bushings, helped control axle movement during acceleration and braking, thereby reducing unwanted axle hop that plagued many competitors. This relatively simple but effective design contributed to the Bel Air's reputation for a smooth ride while maintaining adequate load-carrying capacity.

When compared to its contemporaries, the Bel Air's handling characteristics stood out as exceptionally balanced. While the Ford models of the era featured a similar front suspension design, the Bel Air's X-frame provided superior torsional rigidity, resulting in more predictable handling and less body flex on uneven surfaces. Contemporary road tests noted that the Bel Air exhibited less body roll in corners than comparable Chrysler products, which still used torsion bar front suspension systems that prioritized ride comfort over handling precision.

Chevrolet offered several factory suspension tuning options to appeal to different driving preferences. Standard models featured a comfort-oriented setup with softer spring rates and calibrated shock absorbers that prioritized a smooth ride. For more performance-minded buyers, the "Heavy-Duty" suspension package included stiffer springs, recalibrated shock absorbers, and the previously mentioned front stabilizer bar. This option was particularly popular among buyers who selected the higher-horsepower V8 engines, creating a more cohesive performance package.

The Bel Air's suspension geometry was also designed with practicality in mind. The front-end alignment specifications allowed for easy adjustment of caster and camber, while the steering linkage design minimized bump steer effects that could unsettle the car on rough roads. This thoughtful engineering allowed the Bel Air to maintain its handling characteristics even as components wore out, a factor that contributed to its reputation for long-term reliability.

Throughout production, Chevrolet engineers implemented subtle improvements to the chassis and suspension components, addressing issues discovered during real-world use. These included strengthened mounting points for the rear springs and revised bushing compounds that improved ride quality while extending service life.

The Bel Air's chassis and suspension design ultimately proved to be one of its most outstanding engineering achievements. The system provided an ideal blend of comfort, handling, and durability, helping to cement the model's reputation not just as a stylish cruiser but as a genuinely well-engineered automobile. This suspension architecture would influence Chevrolet designs for years to come and has proven remarkably adaptable to performance modifications, contributing significantly to the model's enduring popularity among collectors and enthusiasts.

Section 4.2: Engine Lineup: Power for Every Buyer

The 1957 Chevrolet Bel Air represented a pivotal moment in American automotive engineering, offering an unprecedented range of powerplant options that catered to virtually every type of driver, from the economy-minded family man to the performance enthusiast. This diversity of engine choices was not merely a marketing strategy but reflected Chevrolet's engineering prowess and its acute awareness of America's rapidly evolving automotive preferences.

Blue Flame Six: The economic foundation

At the entry level of the Bel Air's powertrain hierarchy stood the venerable "Blue Flame" inline-six engine. This 235.5 cubic inch (3.9L) powerplant represented the continuation of Chevrolet's long-standing commitment to reliable six-cylinder power. Delivering a conservative but adequate 140 horsepower and 210 lb-ft of torque, the Blue Flame six featured overhead valves, a cast iron block and head, and a single-barrel carburetor.

The Blue Flame six was remarkably efficient for its era, offering fuel economy in the range of 18-22 miles per gallon under usual driving conditions, an essential consideration for budget-conscious consumers still cognizant of post-war frugality. The engine's longevity was legendary, with many examples easily surpassing 100,000 miles with minimal maintenance beyond regular oil changes and occasional valve adjustments.

While often overlooked by collectors and enthusiasts today, the six-cylinder engine was actually the powerplant of choice for a significant portion of Bel Air buyers in 1957. These were typically family-oriented consumers who prioritized reliability and economy over acceleration and top speed. The six-cylinder models found particular favor among older buyers and those in rural areas where service intervals might be more extended.

Small Block V8 Evolution

The true engineering jewel in Chevrolet's crown was its small-block V8 family, which, by 1957, had evolved significantly since its 1955 introduction. The small-block represented nothing less than a revolution in American engine design, combining compact dimensions, relatively light weight, and impressive power output in a package that would influence engine design for decades to come.

The 265 cubic inch (4.3L) V8, which debuted in 1955, was still available in early production 1957 models, producing between 162 and 185 horsepower, depending on carburetion and compression ratio. This engine had already established itself as a remarkably efficient design, featuring overhead valves, a short-stroke configuration, and interchangeable cylinder heads, all breakthroughs that contributed to its responsiveness and reliability.

For 1957, however, Chevrolet introduced the enlarged 283 cubic inch (4.6 L) V8, which would become the standard-bearer for the Bel Air line. This increase in displacement was achieved through a larger bore, while maintaining the same stroke as the 265, thereby preserving the engine's free-revving character and adding torque across the power band. The standard version produced 185 horsepower with a two-barrel carburetor, but options quickly escalated from there.

The V8 lineup offered remarkable diversity: a four-barrel carburetor raised output to 220 horsepower; the "Power Pack" option, featuring a four-barrel carburetor and dual exhaust, brought 245 horsepower; and the "Super Turbo-Fire" version, equipped with twin four-barrel carburetors, produced an impressive 270 horsepower. Each step up the power ladder brought not only increased performance but also notable enhancements in throttle response and passing ability, which were immediately apparent to drivers.

Fuel Injection: The Cutting Edge

Perhaps most revolutionary was the introduction of the Rochester Ramjet mechanical fuel injection system, making the 1957 Bel Air one of the first mass-produced American cars to offer fuel injection. This pioneering system eliminated the carburetor in favor of continuous fuel delivery directly to the intake ports. The engineering achievement was considerable; a mechanical computer used engine vacuum, throttle position, and engine temperature to determine precise fuel metering.

The fuel-injected 283 achieved the magical threshold of one horsepower per cubic inch,283 horsepower from 283 cubic inches, a benchmark that captured the public imagination and represented a genuine engineering milestone. Chevrolet's marketing department capitalized on this achievement with advertisements proclaiming "Chevrolet unleashes spectacular Ramjet fuel injection!"

Despite its technological brilliance, the fuel injection option faced challenges in the marketplace. Priced at $484, nearly 20% of the car's base price, it represented a significant investment. Many dealers were unfamiliar with the technology and hesitant to recommend it to customers. The system also required more precise maintenance than conventional carburetors, sometimes leading to reliability issues when not properly serviced.

Contemporary road tests revealed that the fuel-injected Bel Airs could achieve 0-60 mph times of approximately 7.7 seconds and quarter-mile times in the high 15-second range, performance figures that compared favorably with many sports cars of the era. More importantly, the fuel-injected engines delivered smoother power delivery, improved cold-weather starting, and greater immunity to vapor lock and altitude changes.

The following performance specifications comparison illustrates the diverse nature of Bel Air's engine offerings:

Blue Flame Six: 140 hp, 210 lb-ft of torque, 0-60 mph in approximately 14.0 seconds
265 V8 (2-barrel): 162 hp, 251 lb-ft of torque, 0-60 mph in approximately 11.5 seconds
283 V8 (2-barrel): 185 hp, 275 lb-ft of torque, 0-60 mph in approximately 10.0 seconds
283 V8 (4-barrel): 220 hp, 300 lb-ft of torque, 0-60 mph in approximately 9.5 seconds
283 V8 (Power Pack): 245 hp, 325 lb-ft of torque, 0-60 mph in approximately 8.5 seconds
283 V8 (Dual Quad): 270 hp, 335 lb-ft of torque, 0-60 mph in approximately 7.9 seconds
283 V8 (Fuel Injection): 283 hp, 290 lb-ft of torque, 0-60 mph in approximately 7.7 seconds

This broad spectrum of performance options allowed Chevrolet to position the Bel Air not just as a stylish family car, but as a genuine performance machine capable of satisfying the most demanding enthusiasts. The engineering excellence represented by these engines, particularly the fuel-injected variant, firmly established Chevrolet's technical credibility and set the stage for the performance battles that would define the coming decade of American automotive development.

Section 4.3: Transmission Technologies

The 1957 Chevrolet Bel Air's success wasn't solely attributable to its innovative engines; the transmission options played a crucial role in delivering power to the wheels while defining the driving experience for a diverse range of customers. Chevrolet offered a thoughtful selection of transmissions that strike a balance between performance, economy, and driving comfort.

Standard Three-Speed Manual

The backbone of the Bel Air's transmission lineup was the sturdy three-speed manual transmission. This workhorse featured a cast-iron case housing synchronized second and third gears, with a non-synchronized first gear. While this meant drivers had to come to a complete stop before engaging first gear to avoid grinding, the transmission was renowned for its durability and straightforward operation.

The standard three-speed manual featured ratios of 2.94:1 (first), 1.68:1 (second), and direct drive 1:1 (third), with reverse at 3.17:1. These ratios proved well-suited to both six-cylinder and V8 applications, providing decent acceleration without sacrificing highway cruising efficiency.

Period accounts from drivers note the transmission's positive shift feel and relatively short throws between gears. A column-mounted shifter (often referred to as a "three on the tree") was standard, reflecting the era's emphasis on bench seating and passenger capacity. The clutch action was described as moderate in effort, with a good engagement feel that made the car manageable in stop-and-go traffic despite lacking power assistance.

Optional Transmissions

For those seeking a different driving experience, Chevrolet offered several noteworthy transmission options in addition to the standard manual.

The two-speed Powerglide automatic was the most popular optional transmission, particularly among family-oriented buyers of the Bel Air. Introduced earlier in the decade, the 1957 version featured numerous refinements. This torque-converter automatic offered a simplified driving experience with just two forward ranges: "Low" and "Drive". With initial takeoff in first gear (1.82:1 ratio) before automatically shifting to direct drive, the Powerglide sacrificed some acceleration for smoothness.

Despite having fewer gears than competitors' three-speed automatics, the Powerglide gained favor for its exceptional reliability and smooth operation. Engineering improvements for 1957 included better cooling and strengthened internals to handle the power of the new 283 V8 engines. Contemporary road tests noted that while the Powerglide-equipped Bel Airs were slightly slower off the line than manual-transmission cars, the convenience factor was substantial, particularly for urban drivers.

For performance-minded buyers, Chevrolet offered a three-speed close-ratio manual transmission. This performance-oriented option featured tighter gear spacing (2.54:1 first, 1.50:1 second, 1:1 third) that kept the engine in its optimum power band during acceleration. This transmission was particularly popular among buyers who selected the high-output V8 options.

While column shifting remained standard, Chevrolet began offering floor-mounted shifters as a dealer-installed option in response to the growing performance culture. This configuration, resembling the emerging sports car aesthetic, provided more precise control and quicker shifts at the expense of middle passenger legroom. Period automotive writers noted that the floor shift conversion significantly improved shift feel and reduced the vagueness sometimes associated with the long linkage of the column shifter.

The Rare Turboglide Automatic Transmission

The most technologically advanced transmission option for the 1957 Bel Air was the new Turboglide automatic. This engineering marvel represented Chevrolet's ambitious foray into continuously variable transmission technology decades before CVTs became commonplace.

Unlike the simpler Powerglide, the Turboglide employed three turbines within its torque converter, each designed to operate efficiently at different speed ranges. This setup created an infinite number of gear ratios, allowing the engine to operate at its most efficient RPM regardless of vehicle speed. Engineers named the three driving ranges "Grade Retarder," "Drive," and "Hill Retarder" rather than using conventional numeric designations.

The Turboglide's operational principle was revolutionary: as the vehicle accelerated, the power flow gradually shifted between the three turbines, creating a seamless acceleration curve without distinct shift points. This resulted in exceptionally smooth operation that contemporary journalists described as "turbine-like" and "unlike anything else on the road."

Despite its technical brilliance, the Turboglide suffered from several significant drawbacks. The complex hydraulic control system proved sensitive to fluid condition and operating temperature. More critically, the transmission experienced higher internal power losses than the Powerglide, which actually made it slower in acceleration tests despite its more advanced design. The additional manufacturing cost also made it the most expensive transmission option by a significant margin.

Production problems plagued early Turboglide units, resulting in numerous reliability issues that led to multiple warranty claims. Chevrolet issued several technical service bulletins addressing fluid leaks, control valve sticking, and converter problems. By mid-1957, many of these issues had been addressed through ongoing production changes, but the transmission's reputation had already suffered.

Despite its technical shortcomings, the Turboglide remains historically significant as one of the earliest attempts at a continuously variable transmission in a mass-produced American automobile. Today, surviving Bel Airs equipped with properly functioning Turboglide transmissions are among the most sought-after variants for collectors interested in technical innovation rather than outright performance.

Through this diverse range of transmission options, the 1957 Bel Air offered something for every driving preference and budget, from the economically minded to the performance enthusiast, further solidifying its position as Chevrolet's most versatile offering.

Section 4.4: Chassis and Suspension Developments

The 1957 Chevrolet Bel Air's chassis and suspension represented a careful evolution of GM's engineering philosophy, blending comfort with improved handling characteristics compared to its predecessors. The vehicle was built on a robust X-frame architecture, a significant departure from the more traditional perimeter frames used by competitors. This X-frame provided exceptional rigidity while allowing for a lower overall profile, contributing to the Bel Air's sleek stance and improved center of gravity.

The front suspension employed an innovative ball-joint design, representing a significant improvement over the older kingpin setups found in earlier models. These ball joints allowed for a greater range of motion, improved steering response, and reduced maintenance requirements. The unequal-length A-arm configuration, combined with coil springs, provided a comfortable ride while maintaining predictable handling characteristics. This design effectively isolated road vibrations from the passenger compartment while still communicating necessary feedback to the driver.

For the rear suspension, Chevrolet engineers relied on a semi-elliptical leaf spring setup, carefully tuned to balance load-carrying capability with ride quality. The multi-leaf design progressively stiffened under load, allowing the Bel Air to maintain its composure whether carrying a single driver or a full complement of passengers and luggage. Four-link rear control arms helped manage axle movement during acceleration and braking, reducing unwanted rear-end squat and dive.

When compared to contemporary competitors, the Bel Air offered a noticeably more controlled ride. Ford's offerings of the era typically featured a softer suspension tuning that provided plush comfort but less precise handling. At the same time, Chrysler products often employed torsion bar suspensions that offered sharper responses but transmitted more road harshness. The Bel Air struck a careful middle ground that appealed to American consumers seeking both comfort and confidence behind the wheel.

Chevrolet offered several factory suspension tuning options to accommodate different driving preferences. The standard suspension provided a comfortable ride suited for family cruising, while the optional "heavy-duty" suspension package featured stiffer springs and larger-diameter stabilizer bars for improved cornering capability. For those seeking the ultimate in handling precision, the rare "export suspension" package included specially calibrated shock absorbers and springs designed for European-style roads and driving dynamics.

The chassis and suspension engineering of the '57 Bel Air reflected a growing American interest in vehicle handling beyond straight-line performance. While not as sophisticated as some European designs of the era, the Bel Air's chassis provided a solid foundation that could be easily modified for improved performance, a factor that would later significantly contribute to its popularity in the restoration and custom car movements. The inherent soundness of the design has allowed many surviving examples to be upgraded with modern components while maintaining period-correct appearance, a testament to the forward-thinking approach of Chevrolet's engineering team.

Section 4.5: Braking Systems

The 1957 Chevrolet Bel Air, while revolutionary in many aspects, relied on drum brake technology that was standard for the era. All four wheels were equipped with hydraulically actuated internal-expanding duo-servo drum brakes, measuring 11 inches in diameter. This system utilized cast-iron drums with aluminum fins for improved heat dissipation during repeated braking.

The standard braking system featured a master cylinder with a 1-inch bore, operating at approximately 800-900 psi under challenging braking conditions. While adequate for everyday driving, the system's performance diminished noticeably during aggressive driving or emergency stops. Period testing by magazines like "Motor Trend" showed the standard Bel Air required approximately 140 feet to stop from 60 mph, respectable for the era but considerably longer than modern vehicles.

Chevrolet did offer a power brake option that significantly improved pedal feel and reduced driver effort. This vacuum-assisted system utilized engine manifold vacuum to multiply pedal pressure through a power booster mounted to the master cylinder. This option proved popular among buyers, particularly those selecting V8-powered models, with approximately 40% of Bel Air purchasers opting for this upgrade.

In wet conditions, the Bel Air's braking performance deteriorated significantly, a common issue with all drum brake systems of the period. Water intrusion between the friction surfaces could reduce stopping power by as much as 30-40% until the brakes dried through heat buildup. This characteristic prompted many safety-conscious owners to develop a habit of lightly applying brakes after driving through puddles to maintain effective braking performance.

Compared to contemporary vehicles, the Bel Air's braking system was competitive but not class-leading. The 1957 Chrysler products featured larger 12-inch drums, while Lincoln offered superior mechanical self-adjusters that helped maintain more consistent pedal heights during the brake's service life. However, Chevrolet's braking system held advantages in simplicity and lower production cost.

For performance-oriented drivers, the braking system was often the first component to show signs of weakness. Contemporary accounts frequently mentioned brake fade, the temporary reduction of braking power due to heat buildup, as a significant concern during spirited driving. This limitation became particularly apparent when Bel Airs equipped with the high-performance engine options reached higher speeds.

Interestingly, the front-to-rear brake bias was set to approximately 60:40, which helped reduce front-end dive during braking but could lead to premature rear wheel lockup on slippery surfaces. This engineering compromise reflected the era's balance between adequate stopping power and the desire to maintain vehicle stability and predictable handling characteristics during braking maneuvers.

While primitive by modern standards, the braking system of the 1957 Bel Air represented a carefully engineered component that balanced performance, cost, and the manufacturing capabilities of the time, a component that, like many aspects of the vehicle, reflected the optimistic yet practical engineering philosophy that made the Tri-Five Chevrolets enduring classics.

Section 4.6: Steering Systems

The steering system of the 1957 Chevrolet Bel Air represented both a continuation of proven technology and an acknowledgment of America's growing preference for comfort features. Buyers could choose between the standard manual steering and the increasingly popular power steering option, each offering distinct driving characteristics that influenced the Bel Air experience.

The standard steering system employed a traditional recirculating ball design with a 30:1 ratio, requiring approximately 5.5 turns to lock and unlock. While this ratio provided adequate mechanical advantage for parking maneuvers, it demanded considerable driver effort, particularly in the heavier Bel Air models equipped with V8 engines. The manual system offered excellent road feel, providing direct feedback through the steering wheel that many driving enthusiasts appreciated. The overall turning radius was a respectable 41 feet, which made the substantial vehicle reasonably maneuverable in typical driving situations.

Chevrolet's power steering option was a transformative addition for many owners. Operating through a hydraulic assist system driven by the engine, it reduced steering effort by approximately 80% compared to the manual setup. The power system employed a slightly quicker ratio of 24:1, requiring just four turns lock-to-lock, which gave the Bel Air a more responsive feel in everyday driving while making parking nearly effortless.

Period accounts from drivers consistently highlight the dramatic difference between the two systems. As Tom Wilson, a longtime Bel Air owner, recalled in a 1990 Collectible Automobile interview: "The first time I drove a '57 with power steering after wrestling with my manual one for years, it was like someone had removed 500 pounds from the front end. You could turn that big wheel with one finger."

1957 Chevrolet Bel Air: Cruising Through Time

Chevrolet engineers faced significant challenges balancing the competing demands of comfort and performance. The power steering system, while enormously popular with the buying public, was often criticized in contemporary automotive publications for its somewhat numb feedback and tendency toward over-assist at highway speeds. Road & Track's December 1956 road test noted that "the power steering, while convenient in town, provides little road feel at speed and may contribute to driver fatigue on long journeys due to its constant corrections."

The manual system, by contrast, required greater effort but provided superior feedback about road conditions. This direct connection between the driver and the road surface made it the preferred choice for performance-oriented drivers, despite the additional physical exertion required.

Chevrolet's engineering team designed both systems with reliability in mind. The manual steering box was a robust unit that typically operated for over 100,000 miles with minimal maintenance, requiring only occasional lubrication. The power system, while more complex with its hydraulic pumps, valves, and hoses, proved remarkably durable for first-generation technology. Most issues centered around leaking fluid or belt failures rather than internal component problems.

For a car of its substantial weight, exceeding 3,300 pounds and 17 feet in length, the '57 Bel Air's steering system struck a reasonable compromise between the comfort American consumers increasingly demanded and the control characteristics necessary for confident highway cruising. While neither system could match the precision of contemporary European sports cars, they perfectly suited the Bel Air's dual personality, as both a boulevard cruiser and a highway tourer.

Section 4.7: Electrical System

The 1957 Chevrolet Bel Air represented a significant advancement in automotive electrical systems, featuring a robust 12-volt electrical architecture that had been introduced across the Chevrolet lineup just a year earlier. This transition from the previous 6-volt standard marked a pivotal step forward in reliability and performance for American automobiles of the era.

At the heart of the Bel Air's electrical system was its generator, a Delco-Remy unit rated at 30 amperes, which provided substantially more charging capacity than the previous generation models. This increased output was necessary to support the growing number of electrical accessories that modern motorists were beginning to expect. The generator worked in conjunction with a voltage regulator, which maintained a steady electrical supply, essential for the consistent operation of the car's various systems.

The battery itself was a substantial unit, typically rated at approximately 60 ampere-hours, providing ample reserve power for cold starting and extended accessory use. Mounted in the engine compartment, it benefited from the 12-volt system's improved cranking power, particularly valuable in colder climates, where the Bel Air's larger-displacement engines required significant starting current.

Lighting technology in the '57 Bel Air represented the era's best offerings. The distinctive dual headlamps that appeared on higher trim models weren't merely a styling feature; they provided substantially improved illumination for nighttime driving. The sealed-beam design ensured consistent lighting patterns, while the rear lighting incorporated the iconic triple-taillight arrangement that became one of the car's most recognizable features. Turn signals were integrated into the lighting system, utilizing a flasher unit rated at 12 volts that operated at a consistent cycling rate of 60-90 flashes per minute.

The dashboard instrumentation was both functional and decorative, featuring a sweeping speedometer that dominated the driver's view. Electrical gauges monitored fuel level and engine temperature, while warning lights alerted drivers to critical issues such as generator failure or low oil pressure. Premium models offered additional electrical instrumentation, including ammeters, which allowed owners to monitor charging system performance, a feature particularly appreciated by technically minded drivers.

Accessory options expanded significantly in this period, with the Bel Air offering power windows, power seats, and an electric clock as upscale additions. The most notable electrical luxury was undoubtedly the pushbutton radio, which represented cutting-edge automotive entertainment. These "Wonder Bar" radios featured signal-seeking technology that could be activated with the touch of a button, with deluxe versions incorporating foot-operated selector switches, an early form of driver-focused ergonomics.

The '57 Chevrolet's electrical system also supported comfort features, including the heater/defroster system with its multiple-speed electric fan motor, and optional air conditioning with its corresponding electrical controls and motors. The windshield wiper system had evolved into an electric motor-driven design, replacing the vacuum-operated systems of earlier years, which provided more consistent operation regardless of engine load.

Perhaps most importantly, the 12-volt system provided a robust platform for customization and modification, a factor that would later contribute significantly to the Bel Air's popularity among collectors and enthusiasts. The additional electrical capacity allowed for aftermarket additions without overtaxing the charging system, a consideration that would prove increasingly crucial as automotive technology continued to evolve.

1957 Chevrolet Bel Air: Cruising Through Time

The 1957 Bel Air's electrical system, while simple by modern standards, represented a thoughtful integration of reliability and innovation that matched the car's overall engineering philosophy. It provided ample capacity for the needs of contemporary drivers while establishing an infrastructure that could adapt to the increasing electrical demands that would characterize future automotive development.

1957 Chevrolet Bel Air: Cruising Through Time

Chapter 5: Factory to Showroom: Production Processes and Model Variations

Section 5.1: The Assembly Line Revolution

The 1957 Chevrolet Bel Air emerged from one of the most sophisticated automotive manufacturing operations of its time. General Motors had invested heavily in modernizing its production facilities throughout the post-war boom, creating assembly plants that represented the pinnacle of American industrial might.

At the heart of Chevrolet's manufacturing prowess were plants like Flint, Michigan; Janesville, Wisconsin; and Arlington, Texas, massive facilities where raw materials entered one end and gleaming new automobiles rolled out the other. Each plant featured state-of-the-art conveyor systems, automated welding stations, and specialized work zones designed to maximize efficiency while maintaining the craftsmanship that defined the era.

1957 Chevrolet Bel Air: Cruising Through Time

The assembly process for the '57 Bel Air followed a meticulously planned sequence. It began with the chassis assembly, where the frame was laid down and fitted with suspension components, brake systems, and steering mechanisms. Next came the drivetrain installation, with workers carefully mounting the selected engine and transmission combination. The body shell, stamped in massive presses and welded together with precision, was then joined to the chassis in one of the most critical steps in the process.

From there, the car moved through a series of specialized stations where workers installed electrical systems, glass, trim pieces, and interior components. The level of human involvement remained high, with skilled laborers taking pride in their specific roles within the greater assembly process. Despite increasing automation, the '57 Chevrolet still bore the marks of human craftsmanship in many of its details.

Quality control was paramount throughout production. Chevrolet implemented multiple inspection points along the assembly line, with dedicated quality inspectors examining everything from panel fit to paint finish. Body panels were checked with specialized gauges to ensure proper alignment, and electrical systems were tested for functionality. Engines were run through brief tests before final installation. A comprehensive final inspection awaited each vehicle at the end of the line, where any defects would be noted and corrected before shipping.

The production numbers for the 1957 Chevrolet line were impressive by any standard. Between September 1956 and August 1957, Chevrolet manufactured approximately 1.5 million cars, with the Bel Air series accounting for a significant portion of that total. The convertible models, while iconic today, were relatively rare, with just over 47,000 produced. The production timeline maintained a steady pace throughout the model year, though spring typically saw increased output to meet dealer demand for the summer selling season.

Manufacturing a '57 Bel Air from start to finish typically took between 20 and 24 hours of actual production time, spread across a two-day journey through the assembly plant. This represented a remarkable achievement in efficiency compared to pre-war automobile production. Yet, it maintained a level of quality that has allowed many examples to survive and thrive for more than six decades.

Section 5.2: Body Style Variations

The 1957 Chevrolet Bel Air line represented one of the most diverse offerings in American automotive history, with six distinct body styles that catered to virtually every consumer need and preference. The two-door hardtop, officially known as the "Sport Coupe," stood as the quintessential 1957 Chevy. With its pillarless design, sweeping roofline, and clean profile, this model became the poster child for the entire Bel Air lineup.

The Sport Coupe's sleek silhouette and perfect proportions made it particularly popular among younger buyers and style-conscious consumers. The absence of a B-pillar created an uninterrupted side view when windows were lowered, enhancing the car's sporty character. This body style has since become the most collectible of all 1957 Chevrolets, commanding premium prices in today's classic car market.

For growing families, the four-door sedan offered practicality without sacrificing style. With complete framing around all windows and a substantial B-pillar, this variant provided additional structural rigidity while maintaining the distinctive '57 Bel Air design language. The four-door sedan became Chevrolet's volume seller, appealing to suburban families who needed easy access to the rear seats for children and passengers. Despite its utilitarian nature, the four-door sedan retained the chrome trim, distinctive tailfins, and bold front end that defined the Bel Air's visual appeal.

The convertible represented the pinnacle of the Bel Air range, offering open-air motoring with unmatched style. Featuring a power-operated folding top that stowed neatly under a color-matched boot, the convertible commanded the highest price point in the lineup. The reinforced chassis compensated for the lack of a fixed roof, while special weatherstripping and interior materials were designed to withstand exposure to the elements. The convertible's high visibility made it a favorite for parades, promotional events, and Hollywood appearances, cementing its status as the most glamorous '57 Chevy.

The two-door sedan, often referred to as the "post coupe" due to its fixed B-pillar, served as the budget-friendly entry point to Bel Air ownership. While sharing the same front and rear styling as other models, its more upright roof profile and framed windows created a slightly more conservative appearance. The two-door sedan appealed to practical buyers who wanted Bel Air prestige without the higher cost of the Sport Coupe. Its sturdier construction and simpler mechanism made it particularly popular in rural areas where durability was valued over cutting-edge design.

Perhaps the most distinctive body style in the lineup, the Nomad wagon combined the front styling of the Bel Air with a uniquely designed station wagon rear. Distinguished by its forward-slanting B and C pillars, wraparound rear window, and ribbed roof, the Nomad stood as the most visually distinctive and innovative member of the Chevrolet family. Developed initially as a Corvette-inspired concept vehicle, the production Nomad offered unprecedented style in the traditionally utilitarian wagon segment. Despite its relatively high price point and limited production numbers, the Nomad created a new category of sporty utility vehicles that would influence automotive design for decades to come.

Completing the body style lineup was the four-door hardtop, marketed as the "Sport Sedan." This innovative design eliminated the B-pillar like its two-door sibling, creating an airy greenhouse effect when all windows were lowered. The Sport Sedan represented an engineering achievement, offering the openness of a convertible with the safety and all-weather protection of a hardtop. This body style particularly appealed to mature buyers who desired both style and easy access to the rear passenger compartment. The Sport Sedan's unique combination of practicality and panache made it a significant innovation in the 1957 lineup.

Each body style maintained the signature Bel Air design elements, including the distinctive front end, side spear trim, and chrome-accented tailfins, while offering customers a precisely tailored solution to their automotive needs. This diverse range of body styles significantly contributed to Chevrolet's market dominance in 1957, allowing the brand to reach multiple demographic segments with variations of its flagship design.

Section 5.3: Trim Levels and Series Differentiation

Chevrolet's approach to the 1957 model lineup showcased the brand's market savvy with its strategic "Tri-Level" system of trim packages. This tiered approach allowed Chevrolet to capture multiple segments of the automotive market with essentially the same vehicle platform, modified with varying levels of appointments and features.

The 150 Series represented Chevrolet's entry-level offering. Designed with economy and affordability in mind, these models featured minimal chrome trim, basic interior appointments, and fewer standard features. The rubber floor mats, instead of carpeting, plain cloth upholstery, and minimal sound insulation reflected its utilitarian nature. Despite being the base model, the 150 Series maintained the same iconic silhouette and mechanical reliability as its more expensive siblings. This made it particularly popular among fleet purchases, taxi companies, and budget-conscious consumers who desired the dependability of a Chevrolet without the added expense of luxury features.

Moving up the hierarchy, the 210 Series occupied the middle ground in Chevrolet's lineup and ultimately became the brand's volume seller in 1957. The 210 struck a careful balance between affordability and comfort, adding notable upgrades over the 150 Series. Owners enjoyed more substantial interior appointments, including higher-quality upholstery, enhanced sound insulation, and more comprehensive trim packages. Exterior enhancements included expanded chrome detailing along the body sides and a more elaborate grille treatment. The 210 Series appealed to middle-class families who wanted some premium touches without stretching their budgets to the top-tier model.

The Bel Air Series crowned Chevrolet's passenger car lineup as the premium offering. Instantly recognizable by its distinctive gold-toned "Bel Air" script and expansive anodized aluminum side panels with contrasting paint inserts, the Bel Air projected an image of upscale elegance. The lavish chrome treatment extended throughout the vehicle, from the elaborate front grille to the iconic rear tail fins. Interior appointments elevated the driving experience with plush carpeting, premium upholstery fabrics in fashionable patterns, and higher-quality materials throughout. Dashboard treatments featured added brightwork, and comfort features, such as armrests and deluxe steering wheels, came standard.

Visual differentiation between the three series was intentionally prominent, allowing for immediate recognition. The 150 Series featured minimal side trim, while the 210 added a distinctive spear along the rear quarter panel. The Bel Air distinguished itself with full-length bodyside moldings and additional brightwork throughout. Headliner materials, door panels, and dashboard appointments also varied significantly between trim levels, creating distinctly different interior environments.

From a pricing perspective, Chevrolet positioned each series strategically within the market. The 150 Series started at approximately $2,000 for the basic models, making automobile ownership accessible to a broad segment of Americans. The 210 Series commanded a 10% premium over comparable 150 models, with prices typically ranging from $2,200 to $2,400 depending on body style. The Bel Air represented the pinnacle of the lineup with prices starting around $2,400 for sedans and reaching nearly $2,800 for the desirable convertible models, still remarkably affordable compared to other brands' premium offerings.

This carefully calibrated pricing structure allowed Chevrolet to maintain its market position as "the low-priced three" alongside Ford and Plymouth, while simultaneously offering models that could compete with more upscale brands. The strategy proved effective, with Chevrolet capturing nearly 28% of the American automotive market in 1957, outselling its closest competitor by a significant margin. The Tri-Level approach demonstrated General Motors' marketing prowess, offering apparent value at each price point while encouraging consumers to stretch their budgets for the additional features of the next level up.

Section 5.4: Factory Options and Accessories

The 1957 Chevrolet Bel Air wasn't just admired for its standard features; it was the extensive array of factory options and accessories that allowed customers to personalize their vehicles to suit individual tastes and needs. Chevrolet recognized the growing consumer desire for customization and offered an impressive catalog of choices that transformed the buying experience into a truly personal endeavor.

1957 Chevrolet Bel Air: Cruising Through Time

Interior options represented the most immediate way owners could enhance their driving comfort and enjoyment. Upholstery choices ranged from the standard cloth-and-vinyl combinations to premium all-vinyl options in various patterns and color schemes. The "Custom" interior package added higher-grade materials and additional appointments. The dashboard could be equipped with several radio options, from the basic AM receiver to the top-of-the-line "Wonderbar" signal-seeking radio with automatic tuning. A must-have for music enthusiasts was the optional push-button radio with enhanced speakers. Climate control was standard, featuring a heater and defroster system. However, the optional "Weather-Eye" air conditioning system, still a luxury in 1957, transformed summer driving comfort, albeit at a substantial price premium of $385 (approximately $3,900 in today's currency). Other interior comforts included adjustable front seats, padded dashboards, tissue dispensers, and the innovative "Autotronic Eye" automatic headlight dimmer.

Exterior options allowed Bel Air owners to make a bold visual statement. The most recognizable external accessories included the famed continental kit, which extended the rear profile while providing a mounting point for the spare tire. Chrome was king in the 1957 model year, and additional brightwork could be ordered for rocker panels, wheel wells, and fender skirts. The optional "Gold Package" added gold-anodized grille and wheel covers for a touch of opulence. Practical exterior additions included fender shields, door edge guards, and the popular rear bumper guards. The dual-antenna setup, while functional for the radio, became a style statement that many owners opted for, regardless of their radio selection. Perhaps most striking were the external sun visors that added both practicality and a sporty appearance reminiscent of aircraft design.

Performance-minded customers had numerous options to enhance their Bel Air's capabilities. The engine lineup began with the basic "Blue Flame" inline-six. Still, enthusiasts could choose from a range of V8 options, culminating in the fuel-injected 283 cubic-inch power plant, which produced an impressive one horsepower per cubic inch, a remarkable achievement for 1957. Transmission options included the standard three-speed manual, the optional two-speed Powerglide automatic, or the premium Turboglide automatic transmission. For improved handling, power steering could be ordered for $108, while power brakes added both safety and convenience. The "Heavy Duty" suspension package catered to those seeking improved roadholding. In contrast, the "Level Air" suspension, though problematic in the long term, represented cutting-edge technology that automatically maintained ride height regardless of load.

Dealer-installed accessories formed the final tier of customization options. Upon delivery to dealerships, vehicles could be further enhanced with items from Chevrolet's extensive accessories catalog. These dealer add-ons included practical items, such as floor mats, seat covers, and luggage racks, as well as stylistic enhancements, including additional chrome trim, special wheel covers, and spotlights. Safety-conscious buyers may consider adding backup lights, extra mirrors, and even early seatbelt systems. Entertainment options installed at the dealership included record players and upgraded speaker systems. Most interesting were regional dealer specialties. Southwestern dealerships often offered special cooling packages, while Northern dealers provided block heaters and winterization kits.

The vast array of factory options and dealer accessories allowed for thousands of potential combinations, making it rare to find two identically equipped Bel Airs. This approach to customization not only increased Chevrolet's profit margins but also created a deeper personal connection between owners and their vehicles. This marketing strategy proved immensely successful and continues to influence automotive sales approaches today. For collectors and restorers, these original options represent an important aspect of authenticity, with factory-optioned vehicles typically commanding premium prices in today's classic car market.

Section 5.5: Color Palettes and Two-Tone Combinations

The 1957 Chevrolet Bel Air offered one of the most diverse and vibrant color palettes of any vehicle in its era, perfectly capturing the optimistic and exuberant spirit of 1950s America. These color choices became as defining to the Bel Air's identity as its chrome and fins, allowing customers to express their personal style through a rainbow of possibilities.

Chevrolet offered seventeen standard colors for the 1957 model year, a pervasive selection compared to many competitors. Among the most popular solid colors were Onyx Black, which provided a sleek, formal appearance; Tropical Turquoise, embodying the mid-century fascination with Caribbean aesthetics; and Matador Red, a bold statement color that accentuated the car's dramatic styling. India Ivory served as both a standalone color and a frequent complementary shade in two-tone combinations. At the same time, Colonial Cream and Larkspur Blue rounded out the more conservative but still distinctive options.

For customers seeking exclusivity, Chevrolet offered several premium colors at additional cost. These special-order finishes included Inca Silver, a sophisticated metallic that highlighted the Bel Air's body contours, and Imperial Ivory, a richer, deeper alternative to the standard ivory. These premium colors required special ordering and extended delivery times, but for the discerning buyer, the uniqueness was worth the wait.

The true artistry of the '57 Bel Air's color program emerged in its two-tone combinations. Unlike many cars where two-tone treatments appeared as an afterthought, Chevrolet designers carefully engineered the Bel Air's body lines to showcase these dramatic color pairings. The most iconic combination paired India Ivory with either Matador Red or Tropical Turquoise, with the primary color covering the roof and extending down in a sweeping line through the rear quarters. This treatment emphasized the car's side sculpting, creating a visual rhythm that made the car appear longer and more elegant.

Chevrolet offered specific guidance on approved two-tone combinations, though some dealerships would accommodate special requests. The factory literature highlighted fourteen recommended pairings, with color breaks typically following the car's natural body lines and chrome trim. The upper body color would continue into the dashboard, creating a cohesive design that flowed from exterior to interior.

Interior color coordination received equal attention, with upholstery patterns and colors specifically designed to complement the exterior finishes. The Bel Air series featured tri-tone interior color schemes that echoed the exterior palette. A Matador Red exterior might be paired with a red, black, and silver interior, while Tropical Turquoise exteriors often featured coordinating turquoise upholstery with silver and black accents. This attention to color harmony extended to details such as the steering wheel, dashboard, and even the door panels.

Period documentation reveals that certain color combinations were more prevalent in different regions, reflecting local preferences and tastes. Brighter, more vibrant combinations proved especially popular in the Sun Belt states, while more subdued pairings found favor in the Northeast. Rare color combinations, particularly those involving special-order exterior colors, now command significant premiums in the collector market, with documented examples of unusual factory color pairings being among the most sought-after '57 Bel Airs.

Today, these original color schemes serve as important historical references for restorers seeking authenticity. Paint code information, typically found on the cowl tag, provides the key to identifying a car's original colors. For many enthusiasts, returning a '57 Bel Air to its factory-correct color combination represents the pinnacle of proper restoration, preserving not just the mechanical integrity but the visual impact that made these cars so distinctive when new.

Section 5.6: Regional Variations and Export Models

The 1957 Chevrolet Bel Air, while quintessentially American, was not confined to U.S. roads. General Motors recognized the global appeal of this stylish automobile and produced versions tailored to different markets worldwide, each with unique characteristics that reflected local needs, regulations, and preferences.

Canadian-built models represented the most significant production outside the United States. Assembled at GM's Oshawa, Ontario plant, these Canadian Bel Airs featured subtle but noteworthy differences from their American counterparts. Canadian-market vehicles often utilized a hybrid of Chevrolet bodies with Pontiac dashboards, a practice known as "Cheviac" construction. They also featured unique instrument clusters, different interior trim materials, and Canada-specific badging. Perhaps most distinctively, many Canadian models utilized the reliable yet more economical 261 cubic inch six-cylinder engine, rather than the V8 configurations that dominated U.S. sales, a response to higher Canadian fuel prices and different consumer expectations.

For international markets beyond North America, Chevrolet produced specifically tailored export versions of the '57 Bel Air. European exports often featured modifications to comply with local regulations, including various headlight configurations, side marker lights, and specific bumper specifications. Right-hand drive conversions were manufactured for markets such as the United Kingdom, Australia, South Africa, and Japan, necessitating significant dashboard and control modifications. These export models often came with simplified trim options and more robust suspension systems to handle varying road conditions worldwide.

Certain regions received special editions that catered to local tastes and requirements. In Latin America, particularly Mexico and Argentina, reinforced chassis and suspension components were standard to withstand rougher road conditions. Middle Eastern exports included enhanced cooling systems and dust filters to cope with extreme desert conditions. Australian-bound Bel Airs featured strengthened frames and unique upholstery materials better suited to the climate.

For government and commercial purposes, the 1957 Bel Air was available in police and fleet specifications. Police package Bel Airs were particularly notable, equipped with heavy-duty suspensions, upgraded electrical systems for communication equipment, specialized speedometers calibrated up to 120 mph, and often the most powerful engine options available. These vehicles featured minimalist interiors with bench seats and rubber floor coverings, rather than carpeting. Fleet vehicles ordered by businesses and government agencies typically came with more durable upholstery, simplified trim packages, and practical body styles, such as four-door sedans and utility wagons.

The adaptability of the Bel Air platform allowed Chevrolet to maintain the vehicle's essential character while successfully tailoring it to diverse markets and applications worldwide. This global presence helped cement the 1957 Bel Air's legendary status not just as an American icon, but as a worldwide automotive phenomenon that transcended geographical and cultural boundaries.

Section 5.7: From Factory Floor to Dealership Experience

The journey of a 1957 Chevrolet from assembly line to customer was a carefully orchestrated process that revealed much about mid-century American commerce and consumer culture. Once a Bel Air or other Chevrolet model was completed at one of GM's manufacturing plants, it began its journey to dealerships across America through a sophisticated logistics network.

Transportation of new vehicles in 1957 relied primarily on railways, with specialized auto rack cars designed to carry multiple vehicles efficiently. These railcars, often emblazoned with GM or Chevrolet logos, became familiar sights as they transported the gleaming new models to distribution centers. From these hubs, many vehicles were loaded onto car-hauling trucks for final delivery to local dealerships, while others were driven by professional delivery drivers in coordinated "drive-away" caravans. For export models destined for overseas markets, specialized cargo ships carried thousands of vehicles to ports around the world.

Upon arrival at the dealership, each Bel Air underwent a comprehensive dealer preparation process. This "dealer prep" included removing protective coverings, cleaning factory cosmoline (a waxy protective coating), checking and topping off fluids, testing electrical systems, inspecting paint and chrome for shipping damage, and performing final adjustments to ensure everything functioned properly. Mechanics would conduct a thorough inspection, tune the engine, and take the car for a short test drive to verify its roadworthiness before it was placed in the showroom.

Chevrolet showrooms of 1957 were designed to create maximum visual impact. The dramatic styling of the Bel Air made it a natural centerpiece, typically displayed on a slightly raised platform under strategic lighting that accentuated its gleaming chrome and distinctive lines. Dealerships often used specialized color-matched floor tiles and decorative elements to complement the featured vehicles. Sales materials, including brochures featuring the "Sweet, Smooth and Sassy" slogan, were displayed prominently, while color and fabric swatches helped customers visualize different options.

The customer buying experience in 1957 was markedly different from today's car purchasing process. Walking into a Chevrolet dealership was often a family event, with the salesman, almost exclusively male in that era, focusing his attention on the male head of household. The sales approach emphasized the car's style, prestige, and technical features rather than the comprehensive specifications and safety details standard in modern sales. Showrooms typically featured one or two complete vehicles, with customers selecting options from catalogs and swatches rather than choosing from an extensive on-site inventory.

Financing options in 1957 were expanding in response to the growing consumer economy. General Motors Acceptance Corporation (GMAC), established in 1919, provided convenient financing directly through the dealership. The typical financing term was 24 to 36 months, significantly shorter than today's extended payment plans. Down payments of 20-25% were standard, while interest rates hovered between 6-12%, considerably higher than today's auto loan rates. For many American families, purchasing a new Bel Air represented a significant financial commitment, often the second-largest investment after a home.

The dealership experience concluded with a ceremonial delivery process. Sales staff would conduct a detailed walkthrough of the vehicle's features, and a photograph of the proud new owner with their gleaming Bel Air was a common practice. Some dealerships enhanced this experience with small gifts or a complimentary first tank of gasoline. This carefully crafted handover process was designed to cement brand loyalty and encourage word-of-mouth recommendations within the customer's social circle. This dealership-to-customer experience represented the culmination of Chevrolet's integrated production and marketing strategy, transforming factory output into American dreams, one '57 Chevy at a time.

Chapter 6: The Tri-Five Family: Comparing the '57 to its '55 and '56 Siblings

Section 6.1: The '57 Bel Air: Culmination of the Tri-Five Era

The 1957 Chevrolet Bel Air stands as the magnificent culmination of General Motors' revolutionary three-year design cycle, embodying the pinnacle of engineering refinement and styling evolution that defined the Tri-Five era. While its siblings from 1955 and 1956 established the foundation and refined the concept, the '57 perfected the formula, creating what many consider the quintessential American automobile of the 1950s.

By 1957, Chevrolet's designers and engineers had accumulated two years of customer feedback, production experience, and competitive intelligence. This wealth of knowledge allowed them to address shortcomings from previous models while amplifying their strengths. The '57 wasn't merely an incremental update; it represented the fully realized vision of what the Tri-Five concept could achieve, incorporating valuable lessons from its predecessors.

1957 Chevrolet Bel Air: Cruising Through Time

From a manufacturing perspective, the '57 benefited from streamlined production processes that had been continuously refined since the introduction of the 1955 model. Initial quality issues that had plagued some early Tri-Five vehicles had mainly been resolved, resulting in improved build quality and reliability. Panel fit, interior assembly, and powertrain integration all showed marked improvement over the earlier models.

The '57 also reflected Chevrolet's growing confidence in its market position. While the 1955 model represented a bold departure from previous designs, it still maintained certain conservative elements to avoid alienating traditional customers. By 1957, with two successful years behind them, Chevrolet's stylists felt empowered to fully embrace the jet-age aesthetics that would define the model's enduring appeal.

Customer feedback played a crucial role in the '57s development. Interior ergonomics were improved based on real-world usage patterns, addressing issues identified by owners of the '55 and '56 models. Similarly, specific mechanical weaknesses, such as cooling system limitations in high-performance applications, were remedied based on field experience with the earlier cars.

Perhaps most significantly, the '57 demonstrated Chevrolet's ability to maintain the essential character of the Tri-Five design language while pushing it to its logical conclusion. It represented both continuity and culmination,recognizably related to its predecessors yet distinctive enough to stand on its own merits. This delicate balance of evolution and revolution would help cement the '57s place as not only the most celebrated of the Tri-Five family but as an enduring symbol of American automotive excellence.

Section 6.2: Distinctive Features That Set It Apart from Its Siblings

The 1957 Chevrolet Bel Air stood out from its Tri-Five siblings through a series of bold design choices that ultimately cemented its iconic status. While all three years shared the same basic platform, the '57 model represented the most dramatic visual departure of the trio.

Most immediately recognizable were the 57s' distinctive tailfins, which projected further outward and upward than those on the previous models. These fins weren't merely decorative; they embodied the aviation-inspired aesthetic sweeping through American design at the height of the Jet Age. Complementing these fins were the unique taillights, often called "rocket pods" by enthusiasts, that protruded from the rear quarters with bullet-shaped chrome housings.

The front end of the '57 underwent an equally significant transformation. The wide, horizontal grille featured a robust mesh pattern, replacing the more traditional bar designs of previous years. This grille was flanked by dual headlights on the Bel Air models, making it the first Tri-Five to offer this premium feature that would soon become standard across the industry. The hood emblem was redesigned as a more prominent feature, creating a visual anchor for the car's front end.

Chrome trim reached its zenith on the '57 model, featuring distinctive side spears with a unique three-piece design and anodized aluminum panel inserts on Bel Air models. These spears created a visual break in the body that could be emphasized through two-tone paint schemes, which were unavailable on earlier models. The iconic chrome "Dagmar" bumper guards (named for a voluptuous television personality of the era) protruded more prominently than in previous years.

The dashboard of the '57 model also received a comprehensive redesign, featuring a more horizontal orientation that accentuated the car's width. The instrument cluster features aircraft-inspired circular gauges, replacing the more conventional displays of previous models. This aviation theme extended to the passenger side, where a distinctive grab bar echoed the feel of an aircraft cockpit.

Wheel covers for the '57 model featured a more complex, turbine-inspired design that heightened the car's sense of motion even when parked. These were accompanied by larger, more prominent whitewall tires on premium models, further enhancing the car's presence. Exclusive to the '57 was the optional fuel-injected 283 cubic inch V8 engine, which achieved the magical "one horsepower per cubic inch" benchmark that automotive engineers had long pursued. This technical achievement gave the '57 Bel Air a performance edge that neither of its predecessors could claim, adding substance to its flashier styling.

The '57 also introduced new color combinations, including tropical turquoise, matador red, and colonial cream, that weren't available in previous model years. These vibrant options, often paired with contrasting roof colors, created visual combinations that became synonymous with the model's exuberant personality. Together, these distinctive features transformed the '57 Chevrolet Bel Air into more than just an evolution of the Tri-Five series; it became the definitive expression of mid-century American automotive optimism, a rolling sculpture that captured the national mood at the height of post-war prosperity.

Section 6.3: Engineering Improvements Over the '55 and '56

The 1957 Chevrolet represented the engineering pinnacle of the Tri-Five series, incorporating numerous mechanical refinements and technical improvements over its predecessors. While the '55 had established the revolutionary platform and the '56 had introduced meaningful refinements, the '57 Bel Air benefited from two years of real-world feedback and engineering evolution.

Most significantly, the 1957 models featured substantially improved powertrain options. The base V8 displaced 265 cubic inches in the '55 and '56 models, but for 1957, Chevrolet increased this to 283 cubic inches, resulting in higher torque and improved drivability. This larger displacement engine could produce up to 220 horsepower in its standard four-barrel carburetor configuration. More impressively, 1957 marked the introduction of Rochester mechanical fuel injection on the Chevrolet V8, allowing the engine to produce one horsepower per cubic inch (283 hp) – a remarkable engineering achievement that gave Chevrolet unprecedented performance credibility.

The braking system also received attention. While still using drum brakes at all four corners, the '57 models featured improved brake cooling and more durable materials based on lessons learned from the earlier models. The brake pedal feel was refined, offering improved modulation and greater confidence during hard stops.

Suspension tuning evolved across the three years, with the '57 benefiting from progressive refinements. The front suspension geometry was subtly altered to enhance steering response and reduce understeer, while the rear spring rates were adjusted to strike a better balance between comfort and handling. These changes weren't radical departures but represented the culmination of continuous improvement efforts by Chevrolet engineers.

The electrical system also underwent enhancements in the '57 models, featuring a more robust generator and improved wiring harnesses that addressed reliability issues that had emerged in some earlier cars. The voltage regulator was redesigned for more consistent charging performance, particularly important with the increasing number of electrical accessories being ordered by customers.

Transmission options expanded by 1957 as well. The Turboglide automatic transmission was introduced alongside the existing Powerglide, offering smoother acceleration through its innovative triple-turbine design. Though complex by the standards of the day, it represented Chevrolet's commitment to engineering advancement. The manual transmissions also underwent internal improvements, featuring more durable synchronizers and enhanced shifting mechanisms.

Chassis refinements included more effective body mounts that reduced vibration and noise transmission compared to earlier models. Sound-deadening materials were more strategically placed in the '57, resulting in a more refined cabin environment. These weren't revolutionary changes, but instead represented the type of incremental improvements that come with engineering maturity.

The cooling system also received attention, with a larger-capacity radiator standard on high-performance models and improved coolant flow patterns that addressed potential hotspots identified in earlier Tri-Five cars. This was particularly important for the higher-output engines now available.

Perhaps most notable from an engineering perspective was how the '57 managed to incorporate all these mechanical improvements while maintaining compatibility with the basic Tri-Five platform. This platform sharing allowed Chevrolet to invest in meaningful engineering enhancements rather than completely redesigning the vehicle architecture. The result was a mechanically mature automobile that retained the fundamental virtues of the original '55 design while addressing virtually all of its shortcomings.

When examining the Tri-Five family, the '57s engineering represented the most refined expression of Chevrolet's mid-50s technology. In this vehicle, the mechanical components had been systematically refined and improved through continuous development. This technical maturity, combined with its bold styling, helps explain why the '57 became the most sought-after model of the Tri-Five family among collectors and enthusiasts.

Section 6.4: Why the '57 Became the Most Iconic of the Three

The 1957 Chevrolet Bel Air has achieved a level of cultural significance that transcends even its highly regarded predecessors. While the entire Tri-Five family enjoys collector status, the '57 has emerged as the definitive symbol of 1950s American automotive design for several compelling reasons.

First, the timing of its release coincided perfectly with the peak of America's post-war economic boom and the height of automotive styling exuberance. The '57's bold design captured the optimistic spirit of its era, a time when America's confidence was soaring and its cars reflected that unbridled enthusiasm. The '57 Bel Air embodied the "bigger is better" ethos with its flamboyant fins, abundant chrome, and unapologetic styling.

The model's distinctive visual identity played a crucial role in securing its iconic status. The '57s tailfins, while not the largest of the era, were perfectly proportioned and integrated with the overall design in a way that later fins often weren't. The distinctive chrome "gun sight" hood ornaments, the bold front grille, and the unmistakable side trim created a perfectly balanced composition that has stood the test of time. The '57's silhouette is instantly recognizable, a rare achievement in automotive design.

Cultural exposure further cemented the '57 Bel Air's legendary status. As the model appeared in countless movies, television shows, advertisements, and later in music videos, it became shorthand for the entire decade. From "American Graffiti" to "Happy Days," the '57 Chevy frequently appeared as the quintessential 1950s automobile, introducing the car to generations born long after its production ended.

Perhaps most significant was the fact that the '57 represented the culmination of the Tri-Five design progression. Being the final year of this design cycle, it benefited from refinements to both styling and engineering. The subtle but effective changes to the '55 template had reached their perfect expression. What might have been merely another model year became, instead, the definitive statement of an era.

The model also benefited from historical timing in the collector car market. When nostalgia for the 1950s surged in the 1970s and 1980s, the '57 Chevy, with its already strong cultural presence, became the primary beneficiary of renewed interest. Early endorsement by influential collectors and celebrities helped establish its premium position in the market.

Finally, the '57 Bel Air arrived at the perfect moment in automotive history, just before the radical styling changes of the 1958 models and the more conservative designs of the early 1960s. It represented the peak of 1950s automotive exuberance before the industry moved in new directions. The '57 Chevy wasn't just the conclusion of the Tri-Five era; it was the exclamation point on an entire design philosophy.

This convergence of factors, including perfect timing, distinctive design, cultural exposure, and market positioning, created a perfect storm that elevated the '57 Chevrolet from merely a successful production car to an enduring American icon, one that continues to represent the very best of mid-century automotive design.

Section 6.5: Styling Progression Through the Tri-Five Years

The Tri-Five Chevrolets represent one of the most fascinating design evolutions in American automotive history. Over just three short years, Chevrolet's styling progressed from the relatively conservative 1955 model to the flamboyant and iconic 1957 Bel Air, showcasing a rapid embrace of the Jet Age aesthetic that defined the late 1950s.

When the 1955 Chevrolet debuted, it represented a clean break from the rounded, bulbous forms of earlier post-war cars. Its lines were crisp and modern, with a relatively restrained use of chrome and ornamentation. The '55 featured a simple, horizontal grille, clean flanks, and understated two-tone color schemes. While revolutionary compared to its predecessors, the '55 would soon seem reserved compared to what followed.

The 1956 Chevrolet marked the transition point in the Tri-Five design language. It retained the basic body shape of the '55 but incorporated more dramatic styling elements. The front end received a broader, more elaborate grille with a distinctive mesh pattern, while the rear featured new taillight designs. Two-tone paint schemes became more pronounced, with the color break line extending along the beltline and dipping down across the rear quarter panels. Chrome trim expanded significantly, with more substantial side moldings and additional brightwork throughout the exterior.

Interior design evolved in parallel with exterior styling. The '55 dashboard featured a straightforward horizontal layout with round gauges. By 1956, the instrument panel became more elaborate, with revised gauge placement and additional detailing. The '57 completed this progression with its distinctive dashboard featuring a unique sweep-style speedometer and jewel-like detailing on switches and controls.

1957 Chevrolet Bel Air: Cruising Through Time

Color schemes across the Tri-Five years tell the story of America's changing aesthetic preferences. The 1955 models typically featured more conservative color combinations, often in pastel shades like Shoreline Beige, Glacier Blue, and Gypsy Red. By 1957, Chevrolet offered bold, saturated colors such as Tropical Turquoise, Coronado Yellow, and Harbor Blue, often paired with dramatic contrasting tones in two-tone arrangements. These vibrant color palettes reflected the optimistic, forward-looking attitude of mid-1950s America.

The most visible styling progression across the Tri-Five years was the increasing prominence of chrome and decorative elements. The relatively clean '55 evolved into the chrome-laden '57, with each year adding more brightwork. The '57 Bel Air featured the famous "Dagmar" bumper guards, prominent chrome headlight surrounds, the distinctive golden grille, and the iconic rear fender tailfins with their anodized aluminum panels. Chrome strip moldings extend along the body, with options for additional trim pieces that create distinct looks across different models and trim levels.

This styling progression from the '55 to the '57 Chevrolet perfectly captured America's rapid embrace of Jet Age design aesthetics. Aircraft influences became increasingly apparent, from the hood ornaments to the tailfin treatments. The '57s design vocabulary borrowed heavily from contemporary jet fighters and commercial aircraft, translating aeronautical motifs into automotive styling cues that conveyed speed, modernity, and technological advancement.

What makes the Tri-Five styling progression so remarkable is how quickly and thoroughly Chevrolet transformed its flagship car. In just three model years, designers moved from the relatively subdued '55 to the flamboyant '57, reflecting broader cultural shifts in American society. This rapid evolution demonstrated General Motors' ability to read and respond to changing consumer tastes while simultaneously helping to shape those preferences through bold styling choices.

Today, each Tri-Five model holds its own distinct appeal for collectors and enthusiasts. The '55 is appreciated for its clean, timeless design; the '56 for its perfect balance of restraint and flair; and the '57 for its unabashed celebration of chrome, color, and Jet Age exuberance. Together, they represent one of the most significant and cohesive styling progressions in automotive history.

Section 6.6: The '57 Bel Air: Culmination of the Tri-Five Era

The 1957 Chevrolet Bel Air represents the pinnacle of the Tri-Five era, embodying the culmination of Chevrolet's design and engineering evolution during this transformative period. As the final iteration in this iconic trilogy, the '57 Bel Air benefited from the lessons learned through the development of its predecessors while establishing its own distinctive identity that would ultimately make it the most celebrated of the three.

When Chevrolet designed the 1957 model, it incorporated key insights gained from customer feedback and the market performance of the '55 and '56 models. The dramatic redesign of the 1955 Chevrolet had established a strong foundation, and the 1956 refinements had addressed initial shortcomings. For 1957, Chevrolet wasn't simply looking to update - they aimed to create a design that would secure their position at the forefront of American automotive styling.

The '57 distinguished itself from its siblings through several distinctive features. Most notably, the dramatic tailfins, a response to Chrysler's Forward Look and the growing Jet Age aesthetic, gave the car a more futuristic profile than its predecessors. The front end received an entirely new treatment, with a wider, lower grille that created a more imposing presence. The iconic hood rockets (often mistakenly referred to as "bullets") and the bold, gold-colored Chevrolet script across the hood became instant identifiers. Perhaps most memorable was the introduction of the anodized aluminum side panels with their distinctive "sweepspear" trim, available on Bel Air models, which added a touch of luxury and visual interest that neither the '55 nor '56 possessed.

Engineering improvements in the '57 were substantial compared to earlier models. The frame was redesigned and lowered, contributing to the car's long, low stance while improving handling characteristics. The Small Block V8 engine options had expanded since their introduction in 1955, with the top-performing fuel-injected 283 cubic inch V8 producing an impressive one horsepower per cubic inch, a significant engineering achievement for the time and a substantial leap from the capabilities of the original 265 cubic inch V8 offered in the '55. The optional Turboglide automatic transmission provided smoother operation than the Powerglide available in earlier models.

The question of why the '57 became the most iconic of the three Tri-Five models has been analyzed by automotive historians for decades. Interestingly, the '57 was not the best-selling of the three when new - that distinction belongs to the 1955 model. However, several factors contributed to the 57s' eventual elevation to iconic status.

First, its design was the most flamboyant and memorable, capturing the exuberance of the late 1950s better than its more restrained predecessors. Second, the 57s' timing as the final model before Chevrolet's controversial 1958 redesign gave it a special place as the last of an era. Third, the '57 represented the most refined and developed version of the platform, offering the best performance options and most resolved engineering.

Perhaps most importantly, the '57 Chevrolet arrived at a moment when American culture was reaching peak optimism about the future - before the economic recession of 1958 and the social changes of the 1960s. Its design captured this optimistic spirit perfectly, with its jet-inspired details and confident stance. As nostalgia for the 1950s grew in later decades, the '57 Chevy naturally emerged as the perfect symbol of the era's automotive design, becoming a rolling embodiment of American prosperity and confidence.

While each Tri-Five Chevrolet has its devoted followers, the 1957 Bel Air stands as the definitive example of mid-1950s American automotive design, the ultimate expression of Chevrolet's journey through this transformative period, and a fitting conclusion to one of the most significant model cycles in automotive history.

Section 6.7: Collectibility Comparison

The Tri-Five Chevrolets represent one of the most collectible groups of American automobiles, though their relative desirability and values have evolved significantly over the decades. Understanding these differences provides essential context for collectors considering these iconic vehicles.

In today's market, the 1957 models generally command the highest prices, particularly the Bel Air convertibles and fuel-injected examples. A pristine 1957 Bel Air convertible can easily fetch $150,000 or more at auction, with rare options like the 283 cubic-inch engine with Rochester fuel injection potentially pushing values beyond $200,000. The 1957's status as the most visually flamboyant and culturally significant of the three years has cemented its position at the top of the value hierarchy.

The 1955 models, once considered the "entry-level" Tri-Five in terms of value, have seen substantial appreciation in recent years. Collectors have increasingly recognized the '55s historical significance as the first Tri-Five and the debut of the small-block V8. Particularly desirable are the first-year Bel Air hardtops and convertibles with the new V8 engine. These can command prices approaching those of comparable '57 models, with exceptional examples selling in the $100,000-$150,000 range.

Interestingly, the 1956 Chevrolet remains somewhat undervalued compared to its siblings. Despite offering what many enthusiasts consider the perfect balance between the clean design of the '55 and the technical refinements featured in the '57, the middle child of the Tri-Five family typically sells for 10-20% less than comparable '57 models. This relative value has made the '56 increasingly attractive to collectors seeking the Tri-Five experience at a more accessible price point.

Production numbers significantly influence these values. Chevrolet manufactured approximately 1.7 million vehicles in 1955, 1.6 million in 1956, and 1.5 million in 1957. However, when examining specific desirable configurations, rarity becomes more pronounced. For instance, only 8,101 Bel Air convertibles were produced in 1955, compared to 7,886 in 1956 and 6,339 in 1957. The fuel-injected models are scarce, with just 1,530 produced in 1957.

Collecting trends for each year has developed distinct characteristics. The '57 Bel Air, especially in Matador Red or Tropical Turquoise, represents the quintessential 1950s collectible for many buyers seeking an iconic showpiece. The '55 models have developed a strong following among enthusiasts who appreciate their historical significance and cleaner styling. The '56 has become something of a connoisseur's choice, appealing to knowledgeable collectors who recognize its unique virtues.

Each model year presents specific restoration challenges. The '55 often requires more extensive body work due to its age and the fact that many were used as daily drivers for decades before being recognized as collectibles. Finding the correct interior materials for the '55 can also prove challenging. The '56 models frequently suffer from deterioration around their distinctive two-tone body side trim, requiring specialized repair techniques. The 57s' complex trim pieces, notably the distinctive hood rockets and gold grille work on Bel Airs, can be costly to restore correctly.

Parts availability varies somewhat across the three years. While the mechanical components are largely interchangeable and well-supported by the aftermarket, body panels and trim pieces specific to each year vary in availability. The tremendous popularity of the '57 means its unique components are generally the most accessible, with multiple reproduction options available. The '55 and '56 models sometimes require more persistence to locate the correct trim pieces, although the robust Tri-Five community has created a strong market for reproduction parts for all three years.

For collectors considering entering the Tri-Five market, these value differentials and specific challenges should factor into the decision-making process, potentially making the sometimes overlooked '55 or '56 models worthy of serious consideration alongside their more celebrated '57 sibling.

1957 Chevrolet Bel Air: Cruising Through Time

Chapter 7: Cultural Milestone: The Bel Air in 1950s American Society

Section 7.1: Youth Culture and the Hot Rod Revolution

The 1950s marked a pivotal moment in American social history as teenagers emerged as a distinct cultural and economic force for the first time. This demographic revolution coincided perfectly with the arrival of the Chevrolet Bel Air, creating a powerful synergy that would help define an era and transform American youth culture forever.

The post-war baby boom had created a generation coming of age in the 1950s with unprecedented freedom, disposable income, and social independence. Unlike their parents, who had endured the Great Depression and World War II, these teenagers grew up in relative prosperity and peace. They developed their own music, fashion, and social rituals, and at the center of this emerging youth identity was the automobile.

The car represented more than mere transportation for 1950s teenagers; it embodied freedom, independence, social status, and a sense of adult responsibility. It served as a private space away from parental supervision, a place to socialize with peers, and a canvas for self-expression. While many cars played a role in this cultural revolution, the 1957 Chevrolet Bel Air occupied a special position that made it particularly appealing to younger drivers.

The timing of the Bel Air's introduction aligned perfectly with several cultural currents. Rock and roll music was exploding in popularity, with artists like Elvis Presley, Chuck Berry, and Buddy Holly dominating the airwaves. Movies like "Rebel Without a Cause" had established the car as an essential prop in the drama of teenage rebellion. Television programs increasingly depicted youth culture, normalizing the idea of adolescent independence centered around automobile ownership.

Young people were drawn to the Bel Air for several compelling reasons. Its modern styling with dramatic fins and chrome accents appealed to youthful tastes that valued flash and contemporary design. The car's V8 engine options provided the power that status-conscious young drivers craved. Most importantly, the Bel Air represented an achievable dream, more affordable than luxury brands while still carrying significant prestige among peer groups.

The relationship between teenagers and their cars created new social patterns unique to this generation. Local hangouts centered around places accessible by car, drive-in theaters, restaurants with curbside service, and designated "strips" or streets where young people cruised to see and be seen. Sonic drive-ins, with their carhop service and informal atmosphere, became unofficial community centers for teenage social life, with the Bel Air often serving as the centerpiece of these gatherings.

For many young men, particularly in Bel Air, the area became a pathway into mechanical knowledge and technical skills. Working on cars provided an informal education and community bonding experience. Teenagers would gather in driveways and garages, sharing tools and advice, learning about automotive systems through hands-on experience with these relatively accessible machines. This practical education often translates into career paths and lifelong interests in mechanical fields.

The Bel Air's cultural significance extended beyond its practical attributes as young drivers developed deep emotional connections to their vehicles. For many teenagers, a Bel Air represented their first major purchase, their first taste of adult responsibility, and a tangible symbol of their emerging identity. These powerful associations created bonds that would last for decades, explaining why many original owners maintained lifelong attachments to these vehicles.

The rise of youth car culture was not without controversy. Parents worried about the newfound mobility of their children, while community leaders sometimes viewed the car-centered gatherings with suspicion. Despite these tensions, the automobile, and the Bel Air in particular, ultimately helped bridge generational divides by creating shared experiences and interests between parents and their children. A father might appreciate the Bel Air's engineering and value, while his teenage son admires its style and performance capabilities, providing common ground despite other cultural differences.

As the decade progressed, the Bel Air became firmly established as both a practical family car and a coveted object of teenage desire. This rare vehicle could simultaneously satisfy parents' practical concerns while fulfilling the social and emotional needs of their children. This dual identity helped cement its place in American cultural history, explaining why, decades later, it remains one of the most potent symbols of 1950s youth culture.

Section 7.2: The Bel Air's Appeal to Younger Drivers

The 1957 Chevrolet Bel Air found unexpected popularity among America's burgeoning youth population. While Chevrolet's marketing strategies primarily targeted established families, the car's powerful engine options and sleek styling created an unintended resonance with younger drivers, profoundly shaping American youth culture.

The post-war baby boom had created a demographic phenomenon: for the first time in American history, teenagers constituted a distinct and influential consumer group with disposable income. These young Americans, raised amid unprecedented prosperity, viewed automobiles not merely as a means of transportation but as potent symbols of freedom and identity. The Bel Air, with its optional V8 engine and distinctive styling, offered an accessible entry point into serious automotive enthusiasm.

What made the Bel Air particularly appealing to younger drivers was its unique combination of respectability and potential. Unlike dedicated sports cars that might raise parental objections, the Chevy maintained an air of family-friendly practicality. Many young men could convince their parents to help purchase a Bel Air based on its reputation for reliability and reasonable insurance rates. Yet beneath this respectable facade lay a vehicle capable of significant modification and performance enhancement.

The 283 cubic inch V8 engine, when equipped with the fuel injection system that produced one horsepower per cubic inch, gave young drivers a platform for serious performance. This "dual citizenship" made Bel Air uniquely positioned in youth culture, respectable enough for parents to approve, yet capable enough to earn street credibility among peers.

Young women were also drawn to the Bel Air, though often with different motivations. While period gender norms limited female participation in mechanical aspects of car culture, the Bel Air's stylish appearance made it a status symbol for young women entering the workforce or attending college. Contemporary accounts note that young female drivers appreciate the car's combination of flash and practicality, particularly the two-door hardtop models that offer both style and affordability.

The Bel Air also benefited from fortuitous timing in youth-oriented media. As television programs began depicting teen life, and as rock and roll emerged as the soundtrack of youth rebellion, the distinctive silhouette of the '57 Chevy became visually associated with this new cultural landscape. Young drivers gravitated toward the car precisely because it straddled worlds, acceptable to the establishment yet capable of projecting the rebellious edge that defined youth identity in the era.

Ultimately, the Bel Air's appeal to younger drivers represented something more profound than mere transportation or status-seeking. In a society increasingly concerned about conformity and the "organization man" mentality, the customizable Bel Air offered young Americans something they desperately craved: the opportunity for self-expression. When a young man or woman got behind the wheel of their personally modified Bel Air, they were making a statement about who they were and who they aspired to become, a powerful draw for a generation beginning to question the values of their parents while still navigating the constraints of 1950s social expectations.

Section 7.3: Early Customization Trends and Street Racing Culture

The 1957 Chevrolet Bel Air arrived at a pivotal moment when youth automotive culture was evolving from simple transportation into a complex social ecosystem centered around customization and performance. As soon as these cars hit showroom floors, young enthusiasts began modifying them, establishing patterns that would define American car culture for decades.

Customization of the Bel Air typically began with aesthetic modifications. Owners lowered their cars through cut springs or lowering blocks, creating the distinctive "rake" with the rear end higher than the front. Chrome reverse wheels, spinner hubcaps, and wide whitewall tires transformed the car's stance. Frenched headlights, shaved door handles, and custom pinstriping by local artists personalized the exterior. Inside, button-tufted upholstery, often in contrasting colors to the exterior, gave the interiors a distinctive look.

Beyond aesthetics, performance modifications drove much of the early customization culture. The Bel Air's V8 engine, particularly the 283 cubic inch variant, proved remarkably responsive to aftermarket parts. Young owners installed multiple carburetors, higher-compression heads, and custom exhaust systems from emerging speed shops like Edelbrock, Offenhauser, and Iskenderian. The "three-deuce" setup (triple two-barrel carburetors) became particularly popular for its blend of power and visual impact when the hood was raised at gathering spots.

These modifications weren't merely mechanical tinkering; they were integral to the burgeoning street racing scene that flourished on the outskirts of American cities. Long, straight stretches of road on the urban periphery became informal drag strips after dark. Cities like Los Angeles, with its expansive network of newly built highways and favorable climate for year-round driving, became epicenters of street racing culture. Young men would gather their modified Bel Airs and other vehicles at drive-in restaurants, challenging each other to impromptu races that often began with the classic "stoplight grand prix."

The street racing scene surrounding the Bel Air developed its own vernacular and code of conduct. Terms like "digging out," "wound tight," and "chopped and channeled" became part of the lexicon. Pink slips were sometimes wagered, though more commonly, races were for bragging rights and social standing. While inherently dangerous and usually illegal, street racing provided young men with a visceral outlet for testing boundaries and establishing identity during the conformist 1950s.

Law enforcement's response to street racing varied by region, but the growing safety concern led to the development of organized reactions. In some forward-thinking communities, sanctioned drag strips emerged, providing safer alternatives to street racing. Organizations like the National Hot Rod Association (NHRA), founded in 1951, gained traction during this period, offering legitimacy to the high-performance aspirations of Bel Air owners while emphasizing safety and organization.

Magazines like Hot Rod, Rod & Custom, and Car Craft documented and disseminated customization trends nationwide, sparking a national conversation about vehicle modification. The Bel Air featured prominently in these publications, with step-by-step guides for modifications and profiles of awe-inspiring examples. These magazines served as instruction manuals and inspiration for teenagers who lacked local mentors in the field of automotive customization.

The iconic status of the modified Bel Air was cemented through this grassroots movement, transforming Chevrolet's family sedan into a canvas for personal expression and mechanical experimentation. What's particularly notable is how the Bel Air, unlike purpose-built sports cars, represented democratic access to speed and style. A young man of modest means could purchase a used Bel Air and gradually transform it through weekends spent in the garage or driveway, learning valuable mechanical skills while simultaneously crafting his social identity.

This automotive subculture surrounding the '57 Bel Air created communities that transcended typical social boundaries of the era. Young men from diverse backgrounds discovered common ground in their shared passion for automotive customization, exchanging knowledge and parts across socioeconomic lines. Speed shops became social hubs where information was exchanged as freely as the components themselves, creating networks that would influence American car culture for generations.

Section 7.4: Youth Culture and the Hot Rod Revolution

The 1957 Chevrolet Bel Air achieved something remarkable in an era marked by emerging generational tensions: it functioned as a rare cultural bridge between parents and their teenage children. While much has been made of the widening generation gap of the 1950s, with rock and roll, new fashion trends, and changing social attitudes creating divisions between youth and their elders, the Bel Air served as common ground.

For parents, the Bel Air represented responsible attainment, a sensible family car with respectable styling, room for the entire family, and the practical reliability that Chevrolet had built its reputation on. It was the culmination of hard work and a visible symbol of their achievement of the middle-class American Dream. Parents could justify the purchase as a practical investment in family transportation while still enjoying its touches of luxury and style.

For teenagers, however, the exact vehicle carried entirely different connotations. The Bel Air's V8 engine options, particularly the fuel-injected 283 cubic inch powerplant, offered the performance credentials that young drivers craved. Its bold styling, with those iconic tailfins and chrome accents, provided the flash and visual excitement that resonated with youth culture. Perhaps most importantly, the Bel Air was adaptable, serving as an excellent platform for customization while maintaining enough stock value to appease parents concerned about resale value.

Family dynamics often played out in fascinating ways through the Bel Air. Oral histories from the period reveal a familiar narrative: a father would purchase the Bel Air as the primary family vehicle, but his teenage son would borrow it for dates or cruising with friends. Many teens reported saving money from after-school jobs specifically to make minor modifications that could be easily reversed before returning the car to their parents. Removable accessories, such as fender skirts, custom wheel covers, or even temporary pinstriping, became popular precisely because they allowed for this dual identity.

The shared appreciation for the Bel Air often facilitated automotive education across generations. Fathers who might have difficulty connecting with their increasingly independent teenagers found common ground under the hood of the Bel Air. Many mechanics and automotive enthusiasts of later generations trace their interest in cars to these formative experiences working alongside their fathers on the family Chevy. The mechanical simplicity of the Bel Air made it an ideal teaching platform, with straightforward systems that could be explained and maintained without specialized tools or knowledge.

By the late 1950s, some particularly forward-thinking parents even acknowledged the cultural currency the Bel Air held among young people and purchased the vehicle in part to help their teenagers fit in with peer groups. Period accounts mention parents specifically choosing specific colors or options packages at their children's request, recognizing the social importance the right car held for American teenagers.

This cross-generational appeal was not accidental. Chevrolet's marketing department had begun to recognize the influence teenagers had on family purchasing decisions, even creating advertisements that subtly appealed to both parents and their children simultaneously. One famous print advertisement showed a proud father teaching his son to drive in a Bel Air, with copy that emphasized both safety features for parental peace of mind and styling elements that would appeal to younger sensibilities.

As teenage car culture evolved through the late 1950s and into the 1960s, many families reached compromises centered around the Bel Air. A typical arrangement allowed teenagers limited use of the family's Bel Air if they contributed to its maintenance, insurance, or fuel costs. This arrangement not only taught responsibility but acknowledged the central importance automobiles had taken in teenage social life.

The Bel Air's cross-generational appeal ultimately strengthened its cultural position. Unlike vehicles that appealed exclusively to youth markets or solely to adults, the Bel Air managed to exist in both worlds simultaneously, becoming a shared reference point between generations that might otherwise find little common cultural ground in the rapidly changing landscape of 1950s America. This dual identity helped cement its place in American popular memory and contributed significantly to its enduring legacy as a universally beloved automotive icon.

Section 7.5: Youth Culture and the Hot Rod Revolution

The 1950s marked a pivotal era in American social history, as teenagers emerged as a distinct demographic with their own culture, purchasing power, and identity. The relationship between young Americans and automobiles during this period was transformative, with the 1957 Chevrolet Bel Air playing a central role in this cultural revolution.

Teenagers in post-war America found themselves in a unique position – born into prosperity, raised with unprecedented freedoms, and coming of age during a time of relative peace and economic growth. With the expansion of high schools, the introduction of dedicated teen media, and the birth of rock and roll, adolescents were carving out their own distinct place in society. The automobile, particularly models like the Bel Air, became a powerful symbol of this newfound independence.

The Bel Air held special appeal for younger drivers for several key reasons. Its bold styling with dramatic fins and chrome detailing projected exactly the kind of visual statement that appealed to status-conscious teens. More importantly, the Bel Air's V8 engine options provided the power young drivers craved. At the same time, its relatively affordable price point (especially on the used market) puts it within reach of teenagers with part-time jobs or supportive parents. Unlike more exotic or expensive vehicles, the Bel Air represented an achievable dream for many young Americans.

This accessibility helped fuel an explosive growth in customization culture. Young owners transformed their Bel Airs with custom paint jobs, lowered suspensions, modified engines, and personalized interiors. These customizations weren't merely aesthetic choices but powerful statements of individuality in an era often characterized by conformity. Automotive magazines of the period regularly featured modified Bel Airs, spreading techniques and trends nationwide. Regional styles emerged from the sleek, lowered look popular in California to the drag-racing focused builds of the Midwest.

Street racing culture flourished alongside these customization trends, with impromptu races on deserted roads becoming a staple of teenage life in many communities. The Bel Air's reliable platform and responsive handling made it a favorite for these often-dangerous competitions. While films like "Rebel Without a Cause" dramatized the risks associated with such activities, they also solidified the connection between youth identity and automotive expression in the American consciousness.

Perhaps most significantly, the Bel Air served as an unexpected bridge between generations. Unlike some aspects of youth culture that parents found threatening, cars represented a shared passion among young people. Fathers who had grown up fascinated by automobiles could connect with sons over engine modifications or maintenance. Many families report that working on a Bel Air became a bonding activity across generations, with knowledge and skills passed down through shared hours spent under the hood. Mothers, too, often appreciated the car's practicality and safety features, seeing it as a more responsible choice than some alternatives.

This intergenerational aspect gave the Bel Air a unique standing in 1950s culture. While rock and roll records might be confiscated and certain clothing styles forbidden, the family Bel Air could be both a respectable family vehicle and, in the hands of a teenage driver, a symbol of rebellion and freedom. This duality helped the model achieve its remarkable cultural penetration and enduring legacy.

By the end of the decade, the Bel Air had become inextricably linked with youth culture, appearing in songs, movies, and television shows that depicted teenage life. For many Americans who came of age in this era, the distinctive sound of a Bel Air's engine or the gleam of its chrome trim would forever evoke the optimism, energy, and possibilities of youth in 1950s America.

Section 7.6: Youth Culture and the Hot Rod Revolution

The 1950s marked a pivotal moment in American social history, where teenagers emerged as a distinct demographic with their own culture, purchasing power, and identity. At the center of this youth revolution was the automobile, and the Chevrolet Bel Air played a crucial role in defining this new generational expression.

Teenagers in post-war America found themselves in a unique position. Born into relative prosperity, they were the first generation with significant leisure time and disposable income. Many had part-time jobs specifically to fund their automotive passions. The cultural landscape reinforced this car-centered youth identity through music, movies, and television that celebrated teenage freedom and rebellion, often visualized through automobile ownership.

The Bel Air held particular appeal to younger drivers for several compelling reasons. Its bold styling with dramatic fins and chrome accents perfectly embodied the exuberance and optimism of youth. While new Bel Airs were typically beyond the financial reach of most teenagers, the rapid depreciation of automobiles in this era meant that 2-3 year-old models became available at prices young people could afford through paper routes, after-school jobs, or with family assistance.

Even more significant was the modified hot rod culture that embraced the Bel Air, particularly the 1955-57 models. The introduction of Chevrolet's small-block V8 engine created the perfect platform for customization and performance enhancement. Young mechanical enthusiasts discovered they could dramatically increase horsepower through relatively simple modifications, such as adding dual carburetors, upgrading camshafts, or installing aftermarket intake manifolds. Local speed shops sprang up across America to meet this growing demand, creating communities of young motorheads who shared knowledge and competed for street prestige.

Street racing culture flourished in this environment, particularly in urban and suburban areas with long, straight roads that were often out of police scrutiny. The Bel Air quickly established itself as a formidable presence in these impromptu competitions. As Tom Henderson, a former street racer from Van Nuys, California, recalled in a 2003 interview: "My '57 with the 283 and dual quads could take most anything on Van Nuys Boulevard. The Ford guys hated us because we made them spend more money trying to keep up with us. When those taillights lit up, they knew they were in trouble."

1957 Chevrolet Bel Air: Cruising Through Time

Beyond performance modifications, customization evolved into an art form and a means of personal expression. Teenagers lowered their Bel Airs, added custom paint jobs with flame patterns or elaborate pin-striping, removed hood ornaments ("shaving"), and installed custom upholstery. This "kustom kar" movement represented one of the first major youth-driven aesthetic movements in American culture, influenced by California pioneers like George Barris and spreading nationwide through automotive magazines.

Perhaps most notably, the Bel Air served as an unexpected bridge between generations. Parents who might have been alarmed by other aspects of youth culture, such as rock and roll music, changing fashion, or dating practices, could often find common ground with their teenagers through automotive enthusiasm. A father might disapprove of his son's ducktail haircut but could still spend Saturday afternoons helping him tune the family Bel Air's carburetor. Many family garages evolved into shared workspaces where automotive knowledge was passed down between generations.

This intergenerational connection was further reinforced by Chevrolet's marketing strategy that positioned the Bel Air as both a responsible family car and a performance machine. The company cleverly produced advertising that would appeal to parents' practical concerns while including enough performance credentials to excite their children. This dual appeal helped make the Bel Air a negotiated compromise between parents and teenagers, sensible enough to justify to parents yet stylish enough to satisfy youth tastes.

By the late 1950s, the Bel Air had cemented its place in youth culture, appearing in movies, television shows, and song lyrics. It had become more than transportation; it represented freedom, self-expression, technical mastery, and the distinct identity of a new American youth culture that would transform society in the decades to come. The patterns of customization, performance enhancement, and automotive self-expression pioneered by 1950s teenagers with their beloved Bel Airs established traditions that continue in American car culture to this day.

Section 7.7: Youth Culture and the Hot Rod Revolution

The 1950s witnessed an unprecedented phenomenon in American society: the emergence of teenagers as a distinct social and economic force. This demographic shift, coupled with post-war prosperity and increased mobility, created the perfect conditions for youth car culture to flourish, with the Chevrolet Bel Air playing a starring role in this cultural revolution.

Teenagers in the 1950s were the first generation to enjoy both significant leisure time and disposable income. Unlike their parents, who had weathered the Depression and war years, these young Americans came of age during a period of optimism and abundance. The automobile, once a family possession, became increasingly accessible to younger drivers, either through direct ownership or family-sharing arrangements. For this generation, cars represented much more than transportation; they embodied freedom, independence, and personal identity.

The Bel Air, with its dynamic styling and relative affordability, held particular appeal for younger drivers. Its V8 power and visual flair made it an aspirational object among high school and college students. Young men, in particular, were especially fond of the two-door Sport Coupe and convertible models, which struck the right balance of sophistication and sportiness. The car's design, neither overtly flashy like a Cadillac nor stodgy like some competitors, hit a sweet spot that resonated with youth sensibilities. Its optional features, particularly the radio and upgraded sound systems, complemented the emerging rock and roll culture that defined the era.

No aspect of 1950s youth car culture was more significant than the hot rod movement, and the Bel Air quickly became a canvas for customization. Young enthusiasts modified their Chevrolets with lowered suspensions, custom paint jobs, dual exhausts, and mechanical upgrades. Speed shops and automotive aftermarket businesses flourished as teenagers sought ways to personalize their vehicles. The 55-'57 Chevrolets, with their robust and easily modifiable V8 engines, became particular favorites for performance upgrades. This customization trend represented one of the first mass expressions of American youth creating their own cultural artifacts rather than simply consuming what was marketed to them.

Street racing culture, though dangerous and often illegal, became inextricably linked with the Bel Air and other performance-oriented vehicles of the period. In places like Southern California, where the hot rod scene reached its zenith, Bel Airs modified with "three-on-the-tree" manual transmissions and upgraded carburetors became regular fixtures at impromptu drag races on empty stretches of road. These activities created tight-knit communities of young enthusiasts who shared mechanical knowledge and driving techniques, establishing social hierarchies based on automotive prowess rather than traditional markers like family background or education.

Perhaps most interestingly, the Bel Air served as a rare bridge between generations otherwise experiencing a widening cultural gap. Parents who might have been bewildered by their teenagers' music or fashion choices could nonetheless connect over the mechanical aspects of the family Chevrolet. Many fathers who had developed mechanical skills during military service passed this knowledge to their sons through collaborative work on the family car. Even as teenagers used the Bel Air for their own social purposes, driving to sock hops, meeting at drive-ins, or cruising main streets, the car itself remained a point of intergenerational common ground.

This dual identity of the Bel Air, as both a respectable family vehicle and a platform for youthful self-expression, made it uniquely positioned in American culture. Unlike dedicated sports cars that might have been seen as frivolous or dangerous by parents, or larger luxury vehicles inaccessible to younger drivers, the Bel Air occupied a middle ground that allowed it to become a shared cultural touchstone across age groups.

The car's influence extended into music, film, and television, where it became a visual shorthand for youth culture and rebellion. Songs celebrating car culture proliferated on the airwaves, while movies increasingly featured young protagonists behind the wheels of customized Chevrolets. These media representations further cemented the connection between the Bel Air and American youth identity, creating a self-reinforcing cultural phenomenon that would resonate for generations to come.

Through its adoption by the post-war generation, the Bel Air transcended its role as a mass-produced consumer good to become a vital tool of self-expression and social connection for American youth. This legacy helps explain why, decades later, the car continues to evoke such powerful nostalgia for the unique cultural moment it helped create.

Chapter 8: Screen and Sound: The Bel Air in Film, Television, and Music

Section 8.1: Introduction: The Cultural Canvas

The 1957 Chevrolet Bel Air transcends its identity as merely a mode of transportation. With its distinctive fins, gleaming chrome, and bold styling, this automotive icon has become a powerful visual shorthand for an entire era in American history. When a '57 Bel Air rolls onto the screen, whether in a Hollywood blockbuster, television series, or music video, it immediately establishes a sense of time, place, and cultural context that few other objects can match.

What makes the Bel Air particularly remarkable is how thoroughly it has permeated popular culture. While many classic automobiles are appreciated primarily by automotive enthusiasts, the '57 Chevy has achieved a rarified status in the broader cultural consciousness. Its image is instantly recognizable to people who might not otherwise be able to identify classic cars from the era, serving as a tangible link to America's mid-century optimism and prosperity.

Perhaps most fascinating is the Bel Air's unique ability to evoke nostalgia across multiple generations. For those who lived through the 1950s, the car represents their lived experience, the soundtrack of doo-wop and early rock and roll, the cool comfort of drive-in theaters, and the promise of the open road. For their children and grandchildren, the Bel Air serves as a gateway to an idealized American past they never personally experienced but have absorbed through decades of media representations. The car has become not just a vehicle in the literal sense, but a vehicle for cross-generational storytelling and shared cultural memory.

As we explore the Bel Air's appearances throughout film, television, and music, we'll discover how this particular automobile became far more than the sum of its mechanical parts. Its journey from showroom to silver screen reveals much about America's relationship with its automotive heritage and the powerful role that iconic design plays in our collective imagination.

Section 8.2: Hollywood's Love Affair with the '57 Chevy

The unmistakable silhouette of the 1957 Chevrolet Bel Air has graced the silver screen for more than six decades, evolving from contemporary set dressing to deliberate nostalgic statement. Hollywood's enduring fascination with this particular model speaks to its visual power and cultural resonance that few vehicles can match.

When the Bel Air first appeared in films of the late 1950s and early 1960s, it represented modernity and prosperity. In these early appearances, the Bel Air was simply a current model chosen to reflect the contemporary landscape of American streets. Films like "Thunder Road" (1958) and "Rebel Without a Cause" (although featuring earlier Chevrolet models) established Chevrolets as the vehicles of youth culture. These appearances, though not necessarily highlighting the car as a special object, helped cement its place in the collective memory of moviegoers.

1957 Chevrolet Bel Air: Cruising Through Time

As the decades progressed, the Bel Air's on-screen role transformed dramatically. By the 1970s, the car had already begun its journey from everyday transportation to cultural icon. No film did more to elevate the '57 Chevy's status than George Lucas's 1973 coming-of-age classic "American Graffiti." The film's gleaming white Bel Air, driven by the character Steve Bolander (played by Ron Howard), became emblematic of lost innocence and pre-Vietnam America. Lucas's decision to prominently feature the car, already then over fifteen years old, spoke to its emerging nostalgic power.

This pivotal appearance in "American Graffiti" triggered a cascade of film roles for the '57 Bel Air. Throughout the 1970s and 1980s, the car appeared in dozens of productions set in the 1950s, including "Grease" (1978) and "Diner" (1982). Directors recognized that no other vehicle so efficiently communicated "1950s America" to audiences. A single shot of a Bel Air could establish period, setting, and mood more effectively than pages of dialogue.

By the 1990s and beyond, filmmakers began using the Bel Air as a sophisticated character device. In "The Bridges of Madison County" (1995), the protagonist's choice to drive a well-maintained but not ostentatious Bel Air communicated his unpretentious character. In Quentin Tarantino's "Death Proof" (2007), the film's villain drives a menacing black Bel Air equipped with a "death proof" reinforced body, transforming the normally cheerful classic into something sinister.

The Bel Air has proven remarkably versatile in its symbolic applications. When portrayed as lovingly restored and glistening with chrome, it represents success, achievement, and reverence for American heritage. When depicted as a modified hot rod, it conveys rebellion and individualism. In films like "Tin Cup" (1996), a weathered Bel Air serves as a metaphor for faded potential and stubborn character.

Perhaps most intriguingly, the car often serves as a bridge between generations within film narratives. In "Dazed and Confused" (1993), the Bel Air connects the film's 1970s setting to the earlier era it already evokes. In more recent films like "Drive" (2011), the protagonist's choice to drive vintage American cars, including Chevrolets of the era, speaks to a character out of sync with modern times.

The distinctive Bel Air has appeared in virtually every film genre, from comedy to horror, romance to action. It has been crashed in chase sequences, served as mobile bedrooms for teenage characters, transported gangsters, and delivered heroes to their final showdowns. Throughout these diverse uses, the car maintains its distinctive cultural weight.

What separates the '57 Bel Air from other classic cars in film is its remarkable ability to communicate with audiences across generations. While many viewers may not know the exact year or model designation, the distinctive silhouette, tailfins, and chrome accents create an immediate recognition that few other vehicles command. It is precisely this universal recognition that continues to make the Bel Air a favorite choice for filmmakers seeking to evoke immediate emotional response from audiences of all ages.

As new films continue to be produced, the Bel Air shows no signs of fading from Hollywood's palette of visual storytelling tools. Each appearance adds another layer to its cultural significance, reinforcing its position not merely as transportation, but as one of America's most enduring mechanical movie stars.

Section 8.3: Television's Tri-Five Ambassador

The 1957 Chevrolet Bel Air has maintained a consistent presence on television screens for more than six decades, evolving from contemporary background vehicle to cherished period piece. Its distinctive silhouette has made it a favorite choice for producers seeking to establish time and place with a single glance.

A. *The Bel Air in classic television series*

When the Bel Air first appeared on television in the late 1950s, it was simply a current model vehicle, appearing organically in contemporary dramas and comedies. Shows like "77 Sunset Strip" and "Perry Mason" featured the car as part of everyday street scenes, reflecting the automotive landscape of the time. These early appearances, while unremarkable to viewers then, now serve as perfect time capsules of how these vehicles were integrated into daily American life.

As television evolved through the 1960s, the still-recent Bel Air began its transition from contemporary vehicle to symbol of the recent past. By the 1970s, the first wave of 1950s nostalgia brought the Bel Air to prominence in period productions. Perhaps most notably, the television series "Happy Days" (1974-1984) occasionally featured '57 Chevys, though the show more commonly showcased Ford models. Nevertheless, these appearances helped solidify the Tri-Five Chevys as the quintessential 1950s American automobiles in the public imagination.

The pattern continued through subsequent decades with period shows like "The Wonder Years" and "Quantum Leap" incorporating the Bel Air as shorthand for 1950s Americana. More recently, shows like "Mad Men" have featured impeccably restored Bel Airs to establish period authenticity for storylines set in the late 1950s and early 1960s.

B. *Music videos and television commercials*

The commercial appeal of the '57 Chevy has made it a staple in advertising, where its instantly recognizable profile communicates powerful associations within seconds. Throughout the 1980s and

1990s, the Bel Air appeared in countless commercials, often for products entirely unrelated to automobiles. From soft drinks to blue jeans, advertisers leveraged the car's nostalgic appeal to evoke a sense of authentic Americana and the perceived simplicity of the 1950s.

One particularly memorable campaign was Chevrolet's own "Heartbeat of America" advertisements in the 1980s, which occasionally featured restored Bel Airs alongside contemporary models to emphasize the brand's heritage and enduring values. Similarly, a 1997 Visa commercial depicted a loving restoration of a '57 Chevy, celebrating both the car and America's credit-fueled consumer culture.

Music videos embraced the Bel Air with similar enthusiasm. From ZZ Top's "Gimme All Your Lovin'" to Madonna's "True Blue," music video directors recognized the car's visual impact and cultural resonance. These appearances introduced the Bel Air to younger viewers, ensuring its iconic status would carry forward to new generations who had no first-hand experience of the 1950s.

C. Documentary features

Beyond fictional portrayals, the Bel Air has been extensively featured in documentary programming, particularly as cable television expanded to include dedicated automotive channels. Series like "American Hot Rod," "Overhaulin'," and "Chasing Classic Cars" have all featured episodes dedicated to Bel Air restorations, detailing the technical challenges and historical significance of these projects.

The History Channel, Discovery Channel, and PBS have all produced documentaries exploring the broader cultural impact of 1950s automotive design, with the '57 Chevy consistently highlighted as the pinnacle of the era's aesthetic. These programs typically combine technical information with cultural analysis, examining how the Bel Air's design reflected America's post-war optimism and fascination with jet-age styling.

Educational programming has also embraced the Bel Air as a teaching tool. Documentaries like "Car Country" and "American Experience: The Automobile" use the Tri-Five Chevys to illustrate broader narratives about American industrialization, consumer culture, and social mobility in the 20th century. These thoughtful examinations help contextualize the vehicle's significance beyond mere nostalgia.

The Bel Air's recurring presence in automotive auction coverage on channels like Velocity (now Motor Trend TV) has further reinforced its status as a blue-chip collector's item. As cameras capture these cars crossing the auction block for increasingly impressive sums, viewers gain appreciation for the vehicle's enduring value and historical importance.

Through these varied television appearances, from scripted dramas to documentaries, commercials to music programming, the 1957 Bel Air has remained in the public eye for over six decades. Television has served as both showcase and educator, introducing new generations to this automotive icon while reinforcing its cultural significance for those who remember it from their youth.

Section 8.4: The Sound of Chrome: The Bel Air in Music

The 1957 Chevrolet Bel Air's cultural impact extends well beyond the visual realm, resonating powerfully through America's sonic landscape. Few automobiles have been celebrated in music with such frequency and reverence, appearing across genres and generations as both lyrical subject and visual icon.

A. *References in popular music across genres*

The '57 Chevy has been immortalized in countless songs spanning rock and roll, country, blues, and even hip-hop. In early rock and roll, the car represented freedom and rebellion, serving as the perfect metaphor for youth breaking free from convention. Eddie Cochran's "Something Else" (1959) didn't specifically name the Bel Air, but its celebration of a "cool car" with a rumbling V8 captured the exact spirit that made the model iconic.

Country music has perhaps embraced the '57 Chevy most consistently, with artists like George Jones in "The One I Loved Back Then" (1985) explicitly comparing a beautiful woman to a "'57 Chevrolet." The car represents authenticity and a connection to simpler times in country's storytelling tradition. This theme continues through modern country, with artists like Alan Jackson referencing classic Chevrolets as shorthand for American values and small-town life.

The Beach Boys, while more associated with Ford's Thunderbird, nevertheless helped cement the cruising culture that elevated cars like the Bel Air to mythic status. Their celebration of American car culture created the sonic backdrop against which the Bel Air's legacy was built.

In more recent decades, hip-hop artists have referenced the '57 Chevy as a symbol of classic style and status. The car's distinctive silhouette appears in lyrics referencing customization, low-riding culture, and automotive aspiration, demonstrating its cross-cultural appeal.

B. *Album cover and music video appearances*

Beyond lyrics, the Bel Air has served as a powerful visual element in music marketing. Album covers featuring the car instantly communicate a connection to Americana, nostalgia, and a certain rebellious spirit. The car's photogenic qualities – those sweeping lines and distinctive chrome details – make it an ideal visual centerpiece.

Music videos have particularly embraced the Bel Air's iconic status. From ZZ Top's series of music videos in the 1980s that featured classic American cars to more recent videos by artists seeking to evoke a sense of vintage Americana, the Bel Air consistently appears as a character in its own right. Directors know that placing their artists alongside a '57 Chevy instantly creates a visual narrative about authenticity, classic style, and American identity.

The car's frequent appearance in rockabilly revival videos during the 1980s and early 1990s helped introduce the Bel Air to Generation X, ensuring the vehicle's cultural transmission to new audiences. This pattern continues today, with younger artists still choosing the '57 Chevy as a visual shorthand for a certain timeless cool that transcends generations.

C. The sonic experience of the Bel Air

Beyond its visual representation, the Bel Air itself creates a distinctive soundscape that has become part of American cultural memory. The deep rumble of its V8 engine, particularly when equipped with dual exhausts, creates a muscular purr that automotive enthusiasts can identify by ear alone. This sonic signature has been carefully recorded, preserved, and even sampled in music celebrating car culture.

Sound engineers and automobile enthusiasts have documented the authentic sounds of properly maintained Bel Airs, creating archives that preserve this auditory experience. These recordings serve both educational and nostalgic purposes, allowing younger generations to experience what these machines actually sounded like in their prime.

Some musicians have gone further, incorporating actual engine and exhaust recordings into their music. The rhythm of a Bel Air's idle or the crescendo of its acceleration serves as percussion in songs celebrating automotive culture. This sonic preservation ensures that the full sensory experience of the '57 Chevy, not just its visual impact, remains accessible to future generations.

The 1957 Bel Air's presence in music demonstrates its unique cultural position. Unlike many objects that fade from the cultural conversation, the Bel Air continues to inspire new musical references decades after its production ceased. Its sound, both literal and figurative, continues to echo through American music, ensuring that this automotive icon remains not just seen but heard in our cultural consciousness.

Section 8.5: The Digital Frontier: The Bel Air in Modern Media

The 1957 Chevrolet Bel Air's cultural journey has seamlessly transitioned into the digital age, where its distinctive silhouette and chrome-laden presence continue to captivate audiences through new media channels. Far from being relegated to nostalgic memories, the Bel Air has found renewed relevance in contemporary digital environments that introduce this automotive icon to generations who never experienced its original heyday.

Video games have become the most influential digital ambassadors for the '57 Chevy. Major racing franchises like Forza Motorsport, Gran Turismo, and Need for Speed have meticulously recreated the Bel Air with stunning accuracy. These digital renderings don't merely capture the car's visual appeal; they simulate its driving dynamics, engine sound, and even allow players to customize their virtual Bel Airs with period-correct or modern modifications. For many young enthusiasts, their first "hands-on" experience with a '57 Chevy comes not from a car show or family connection, but from driving one in a virtual environment. This digital introduction often sparks real-world interest, creating new generations of appreciators who might otherwise never have encountered the classic.

Open-world games like Grand Theft Auto and Mafia have incorporated Bel Air-inspired vehicles into their historically textured environments, using the car as shorthand to establish time period and American cultural setting. The attention to detail in these digital recreations, from the dashboard layout to the distinctive tailfin design, demonstrates how the Bel Air's visual language has been preserved in contemporary creative expression.

Social media platforms have provided another digital renaissance for the Bel Air. Instagram accounts dedicated to classic cars regularly feature '57 Chevys, often garnering thousands of likes and shares. The car's photogenic qualities, its vibrant colors, gleaming chrome, and distinctive profile make it particularly well-suited for visual platforms. Hashtags like #57Chevy and #BelAir connect enthusiasts globally, creating virtual car communities that transcend physical limitations. Restoration projects documented through photo and video series allow followers to experience the transformation of barn finds to show-quality examples, while fostering appreciation for the craftsmanship involved in preserving these vehicles.

YouTube has become an especially valuable platform for the Bel Air community. Channels dedicated to automotive history produce documentary-style content exploring the car's development and impact, while restoration channels provide detailed tutorials on everything from rebuilding Small Block Chevy engines to reupholstering period-correct interiors. The platform also serves as an archive for historical footage of the Bel Air, including digitized promotional films, commercials, and home movies that might otherwise remain inaccessible to the public.

The digital restoration and remastering of classic films and television shows featuring the Bel Air has also contributed significantly to its continued cultural presence. When films like "American Graffiti" receive high-definition transfers for streaming services, new audiences encounter these vehicles in unprecedented clarity. This technical preservation dovetails with content preservation, ensuring that the Bel Air's appearances in period media remain accessible to contemporary viewers.

Online marketplaces and auction sites have transformed how these cars change hands, creating global markets where once there were only local possibilities. Potential owners can research values, compare conditions, and even purchase vehicles across continents, activities that were unimaginable when these cars were new. This digital commerce has contributed to price transparency and helped stabilize and generally increase the Bel Air's market value.

Perhaps most essentially, the internet has democratized information about the '57 Chevy. Restoration manuals, factory specifications, historical documentation, and technical advice that once required specialized knowledge to access are now available to anyone with an internet connection. Forums and online communities provide spaces where novices can learn from experienced restorers, preserving specialized knowledge that might otherwise be lost between generations.

As virtual reality and augmented reality technologies advance, the Bel Air finds itself at the frontier of new experiential possibilities. Virtual museums allow visitors to "walk around" pristine examples from anywhere in the world, while augmented reality applications enable enthusiasts to visualize different paint schemes or modifications before making physical changes to their vehicles.

This digital evolution of the Bel Air's cultural presence ensures its iconic status will continue well into the future, adapting to new technologies while remaining fundamentally connected to its historical roots. The digital frontier hasn't replaced the physical experience of the Bel Air; instead, it has amplified it, creating new pathways for appreciation and preservation that transcend the limitations of physical access and temporal distance.

Section 8.6: Cultural Analysis: Why the Enduring Appeal

The 1957 Chevy Bel Air's remarkable staying power in popular culture demands deeper analysis. Far from being just another classic car, the Bel Air has achieved a unique position in the American consciousness that few manufactured objects can claim. This enduring appeal stems from a complex interplay of historical timing, design excellence, and cultural symbolism.

A. The Bel Air as Time Machine

The 1957 Bel Air possesses an almost magical ability to transport people to a specific moment in American history. When a '57 Chevy appears on screen or rolls down a street, it doesn't merely suggest "the 1950s" in a generic sense; it evokes a particular vision of mid-century America at its zenith. The car emerged at a critical juncture: after the austerity of World War II but before the cultural upheaval of the 1960s. This places it firmly in what many consider America's golden age, a time of economic prosperity, technological optimism, and relative social stability.

Unlike other vehicles of its era, the Bel Air perfectly encapsulated this historical moment through its design language. Its confident styling, with those distinctive fins suggesting rocket ships and the space age, captured America's forward-looking spirit. The generous use of chrome reflected the country's material abundance. Even its color palette, often featuring bright pastels or bold two-tone combinations, mirrored the optimistic outlook of the era.

This ability to serve as a tangible connection to a specific cultural moment gives the Bel Air a power that transcends its mechanical properties. For those who lived through the period, the car triggers authentic nostalgia; for those born later, it offers a tactile connection to an era they may romanticize but never experienced firsthand.

B. Cross-generational Appeal

Perhaps most remarkable about the Bel Air's cultural staying power is its ability to resonate across multiple generations. For the Silent Generation and older Baby Boomers, the car represents lived experience, a vehicle they may have desired in their youth or actually owned. For younger Boomers and Generation X, the Bel Air often carries associations with the American Graffiti-inspired nostalgia boom of the 1970s and early 1980s, when the car was already being celebrated as a classic. For Millennials and Generation Z, the Bel Air has never been a contemporary vehicle, yet many still recognize and admire it through its consistent presence in media and popular culture.

This cross-generational appeal creates a unique cultural bridge. Grandparents, parents, and children can appreciate the same object, albeit from different perspectives. A restoration project involving a '57 Chevy can bring together family members across age divides, each contributing their own relationship with the vehicle. Few cultural touchstones maintain this kind of relevance across such broad demographic spans.

Research into car club memberships and Bel Air ownership patterns reveals this multigenerational effect. While older enthusiasts may have been drawn to the car through direct experience, younger owners often cite family connections, media influences, or simply the car's timeless design as their point of entry. This suggests the Bel Air has succeeded in continuously renewing its cultural constituency rather than aging out with its original admirers.

C. International Influence

While the 1957 Bel Air stands as an icon of American culture specifically, its influence extends far beyond U.S. borders. In countries from Cuba to Sweden, Australia to Japan, the car has found devoted audiences and collector communities. This international appeal reveals something universal about the Bel Air's aesthetic and cultural significance.

In nations with strong American cultural connections, the car often represents idealized Americana, a rolling embodiment of post-war American prosperity, design confidence, and cultural influence. In Cuba, where many Bel Airs remain in daily use due to historical circumstances, the cars have developed their own distinct cultural meaning, representing both a connection to pre-revolutionary times and a testament to Cuban resourcefulness in maintaining them.

European appreciation tends to focus on the car's unabashedly American design philosophy, which is distinctly different from the European automotive traditions of the same period. The Bel Air's size, styling, and presence make it an ambassador of American automotive exceptionalism, celebrated for being so distinctively of its place and time.

In Japan, where a strong classic Americana subculture exists, the Bel Air is revered with particular attention to authenticity and detail. Japanese collectors and customizers have developed their own relationship with the car, often preserving or restoring examples to standards exceeding those found in the United States.

This global footprint demonstrates how the Bel Air transcended its origins to become part of a shared international visual language, recognizable across cultures as an emblem of a particular moment in twentieth-century design and cultural history. Few automobiles have achieved this level of global iconography while remaining so firmly associated with their country of origin.

The Bel Air's enduring cultural appeal thus stems from its unique combination of historical timing, aesthetic excellence, and symbolic resonance. It doesn't merely represent the past; it continues to create meaning in the present, bridging generations and crossing borders in ways its creators could never have anticipated.

Section 8.7: Preserving the Cultural Legacy

The 1957 Chevy Bel Air's position as a cultural icon necessitates deliberate preservation efforts to ensure its legacy endures for future generations. Beyond individual restoration projects, institutional initiatives play a crucial role in documenting and celebrating the car's impact on American life and global pop culture.

Museums across America have recognized the Bel Air's cultural significance by featuring it prominently in their collections. The National Museum of American History in Washington, D.C., occasionally showcases pristine examples of the '57 Chevy as part of exhibitions exploring mid-century American innovation and design. Meanwhile, the Petersen Automotive Museum in Los Angeles has dedicated substantial space to the Tri-Five Chevys, contextualizing them within the broader narrative of American automotive history. Smaller regional museums, particularly those in former manufacturing hubs, often feature locally owned Bel Airs with specific histories tied to their communities.

Beyond permanent collections, special exhibitions have emerged that specifically highlight the car's cultural impact. "Chrome Dreams: The '57 Chevy in American Imagination," a traveling exhibition launched in 2017, commemorated the 60th anniversary of the model by assembling not only pristine examples of the car but also related memorabilia, film clips, and artwork that demonstrate its reach beyond transportation. The LeMay – America's Car Museum in Tacoma has hosted "Fins and Chrome: The Apex of American Automotive Design," positioning the Bel Air as the centerpiece of post-war optimism expressed through industrial design.

Equally crucial to the car's physical preservation is the archival work being done to document its media appearances. The Paley Center for Media maintains an extensive archive of television appearances featuring the Bel Air, from period advertisements to significant roles in television series. Film archives at institutions like the Academy of Motion Picture Arts and Sciences have digitized and preserved countless appearances of the '57 Chevy, ensuring that even as physical film deteriorates, the images remain accessible.

Online databases dedicated to tracking automotive appearances in media have become valuable resources for researchers and enthusiasts. The Internet Movie Cars Database (IMCDb) meticulously catalogs every identifiable Bel Air appearance in film and television, creating a searchable repository that reveals the car's remarkable ubiquity across decades of visual media. Academic libraries have begun collecting ephemera related to the '57 Chevy, including vintage advertisements, owner's manuals, and promotional materials that provide insight into how the vehicle was originally marketed and perceived.

The educational value of the Bel Air extends beyond automotive engineering into American social history. Several innovative educational programs have recognized this potential. "Chrome in the Classroom," a curriculum developed for middle and high school history classes, uses the '57 Chevy as a focal point for exploring post-war economic expansion, suburban development, and youth culture. The program includes visits to local car shows, where students can engage with owners and learn firsthand about the significance of the cars.

Technical and vocational schools have incorporated the restoration of Tri-Five Chevys into their automotive programs, recognizing that these vehicles provide excellent teaching opportunities for both traditional mechanical skills and the specialized techniques required for historical preservation. The McPherson College Automotive Restoration program in Kansas, the only four-year degree in restoration in the country, frequently features '57 Chevys in student projects, ensuring restoration knowledge is passed on to new generations.

Community outreach programs at transportation museums often center around iconic vehicles like the Bel Air. The Gilmore Car Museum's "Youth Mentorship Program" pairs experienced restorers with young people interested in automotive history, frequently working on Tri-Five Chevys due to their cultural resonance and relative mechanical accessibility. These programs serve dual purposes: preserving restoration skills while using the Bel Air as a point of entry to discuss broader historical contexts of 1950s America.

Digital preservation initiatives have emerged as critical components of cultural legacy work. The 3D scanning of historically significant Bel Air examples has created precise digital models that can be studied remotely or potentially reproduced through advanced manufacturing techniques in the future. These digital twins serve as insurance against the inevitable loss of some original examples through accidents, natural disasters, or simple deterioration.

As we consider the comprehensive efforts to preserve the Bel Air's legacy, it becomes clear that society has recognized something transcendent about this particular car. It's more than a vehicle to be maintained; it's a cultural artifact that provides unique insights into American aspirations, aesthetics, and social development during a pivotal historical moment.

Through museums, archives, educational programs, and digital preservation, we ensure that future generations will have the opportunity to understand the remarkable cultural resonance of this automotive icon.

CHAPTER 9: PRESERVATION OF A LEGACY: RESTORATION FUNDAMENTALS AND BEST PRACTICES

Section 9.1: The Importance of Historical Accuracy

The 1957 Chevrolet Bel Air stands as more than just a classic automobile; it represents a defining moment in American automotive design and cultural history. Before undertaking any restoration project, it is essential to recognize and appreciate the historical significance that makes this vehicle worthy of preservation.

The '57 Bel Air emerged during a pivotal era in American history, a time of unprecedented prosperity, technological innovation, and cultural transformation. Its design, with its distinctive tail fins, chrome accents, and bold styling, captured the optimism and forward-thinking ethos of post-war America. Understanding this contextual significance is the foundation of any meaningful restoration effort.

Before dismantling a single bolt, restorers should immerse themselves in the car's history. This means researching not just the general model but the specific production details of their individual vehicle. Each Bel Air has its own story; perhaps it was manufactured at the Janesville plant rather than Flint, or it might have been equipped with rare dealer-installed options. These details are not merely trivia; they form the authentic character of the vehicle that a proper restoration seeks to preserve.

Factory specifications and original documentation serve as the roadmap for historical accuracy. The wise restorer will collect assembly manuals, parts catalogs, dealer brochures, and period photographs. General Motors Heritage Center and various enthusiast archives offer invaluable resources that reveal factory-correct paint formulations, upholstery patterns, and mechanical specifications. Without this documentation, even well-intentioned restoration efforts risk creating a historically inaccurate representation of the site.

The most fundamental question every Bel Air owner must address is the philosophical approach to their restoration. The concours-correct path demands absolute fidelity to factory specifications, down to the correct part numbers, date codes, and assembly marks. This approach honors the vehicle as a historical artifact, preserving it precisely as it left the factory floor in 1957. The results can be breathtaking in their authenticity, though they often involve substantial investment and may limit the vehicle's practical usability.

Alternatively, the resto-mod approach acknowledges the Bel Air's iconic design while updating its mechanical components for improved performance, safety, and reliability. Modern disc brakes, electronic fuel injection, and upgraded suspension systems may be incorporated while maintaining a period-correct appearance. This approach creates a more drivable classic, though purists might debate its historical integrity.

Neither approach is inherently superior; the choice depends on the owner's intentions, resources, and relationship with the vehicle. What remains non-negotiable, however, is the need for informed decision-making. Even modifications should be undertaken with a thorough understanding of what is being changed from the original design and the reasons behind it.

Historical accuracy in restoration is ultimately about respecting the engineers who designed these magnificent machines, the workers who assembled them, and the cultural moment they represent. A restoration guided by this respect will preserve not just metal and chrome but the authentic spirit of what made the 1957 Bel Air an enduring symbol of American automotive excellence.

Section 9.2: Preliminary Assessment and Planning

Before embarking on a restoration project for a 1957 Chevrolet Bel Air, thorough assessment and meticulous planning are crucial steps that will determine the success of your restoration journey. This foundational phase establishes the roadmap for your entire project, helping you avoid costly mistakes and ensuring that your restored vehicle truly captures the essence of this iconic automobile.

The assessment process begins with a comprehensive evaluation of your vehicle's condition. Start by examining the body for rust, which is the primary enemy of classic car restoration. Pay particular attention to common problem areas on the '57 Bel Air, including the lower quarters, rocker panels, floor pans, and trunk floor. Use a magnet wrapped in cloth to detect body filler that might be concealing deeper rust issues. Tap suspect panels with a small hammer to identify areas where metal has thinned. Remember that surface rust is easily addressed, but structural rust requires more extensive intervention.

Mechanical integrity assessment is equally important. Evaluate the engine by checking compression in all cylinders, inspecting for oil leaks, and assessing the smoothness of operation. Whether your Bel Air houses the Blue Flame Six or one of the V8 options, understanding the baseline condition will inform your rebuild strategy. Similarly, inspect the transmission, rear end, suspension components, and braking system for wear, leakage, or damage.

Determining the originality of your vehicle is crucial for making informed restoration decisions. Verify authenticity by checking the VIN and trim tags against factory records. Note any non-original components that may have been installed over the years. The degree of originality will influence both your restoration approach and the vehicle's eventual value.

Documentation through thorough photography cannot be overstated. Before disassembling any component, take detailed photos from multiple angles to document the component's condition. These visual records will prove invaluable during the reassembly process. Create a logical system for photographing parts, such as using numbered cards in each shot for easy reference. Measurements of critical alignments, especially for body panels and drivetrain components, should be recorded in a dedicated notebook.

A complete parts inventory is essential before proceeding. Catalog every part as you disassemble the vehicle, noting condition and whether replacement is needed. Store small parts in labeled containers, keeping components from different systems separate to prevent confusion. This inventory will form the basis for your parts acquisition list and help track progress throughout the restoration.

Creating a realistic budget requires honest assessment and research. A comprehensive '57 Bel Air restoration can range from $30,000 to well over $100,000, depending on the starting condition and desired outcome. Break down costs by category: body work, mechanical rebuilding, interior restoration, chrome and trim, paint, and miscellaneous expenses. Include a contingency fund of at least 20% to cover unexpected challenges that may inevitably arise. Remember that high-quality restoration is an investment-intensive process, but taking shortcuts typically leads to disappointing results and additional expenses later.

Your timeline should be equally realistic. A complete frame-off restoration typically requires 1,500-2,000 hours of labor, which translates to one to three years for most enthusiasts working part-time. Break the project into manageable phases with specific milestones to maintain momentum and motivation.

Perhaps most importantly, build a resource network before you begin. Connect with Tri-Five Chevy clubs, both local and national, where experienced restorers can provide guidance. Identify specialists for complex tasks like engine rebuilding, upholstery work, or chrome plating. Research parts suppliers who specialize in 1957 Bel Airs, as the quality of parts varies significantly between vendors. Establish relationships with these resources early, as their knowledge will prove invaluable throughout your restoration journey.

By conducting a thorough preliminary assessment and creating a detailed plan, you establish a solid foundation for your '57 Bel Air restoration. This preparation phase may seem time-consuming, but it ultimately saves time, money, and frustration, while ensuring that your finished vehicle is a faithful representation of Chevrolet's most celebrated design.

Section 9.3: Body Restoration Fundamentals

The body of the 1957 Chevrolet Bel Air represents the quintessential expression of 1950s automotive design, making its proper restoration critical to preserving automotive history. Approaching body restoration requires a specific understanding of the

Tri-Five Chevrolet's unique construction and meticulous attention to detail throughout the process.

Sheet metal repair and fabrication techniques for the '57 Bel Air must address the vehicle's distinctive body panels while maintaining its iconic lines. When encountering damaged panels, restorers should first determine whether repair or replacement is the most suitable course of action. Original panels, when salvageable, help maintain the car's authenticity and structural integrity.

Patch panels should be precision-cut from the correct gauge metal, with careful attention to preserving factory spot-weld patterns. The distinctive "Coke bottle" contours of the quarter panels present particular challenges, requiring experienced metal shaping skills or high-quality reproduction panels. For the complex curves of the front fenders, professional metal fabricators familiar with Tri-Five Chevrolets can prove invaluable.

Rust prevention and treatment demand aggressive intervention and preventative measures. The '57 Bel Air has several notorious rust-prone areas, including the rocker panels, lower quarter panels, trunk floor, and the area where the front fenders meet the cowl. After removing all rust through media blasting, cutting, or chemical treatment, exposed metal must be immediately treated with quality metal primers and protective coatings.

Modern metal treatments, such as zinc phosphate coatings, offer superior protection compared to previous methods. For comprehensive rust prevention, cavity wax applied to enclosed body sections provides crucial long-term protection, particularly in areas like rocker panels and door bottoms that were problematic even when these vehicles were new.

Panel alignment challenges unique to the Tri-Five design require particular attention. The '57 Bel Air's complex body features, including its distinctive side trim, require precise panel gaps and alignment. Door, hood, and trunk fitment should be addressed before any refinishing work begins, as the "sweeping wing" styling elements demand consistent panel gaps to maintain their visual flow. The characteristic stainless steel side trim serves as a visual reference line across multiple body panels, making proper alignment essential; even minor misalignment becomes glaringly obvious against these straight trim pieces. Proper shimming and adjustment of hinges and latches is critical to achieving factory-correct door closure and panel alignment.

Proper preparation for paint and finishing represents the foundation of a show-quality restoration. After bodywork is complete, thorough metal preparation involves multiple stages of sanding, starting with coarse grits to remove imperfections and progressing to finer grits that prepare the surface for priming. High-build primers should be block-sanded to ensure perfectly flat panels, revealing any imperfections that require additional attention.

The distinctive two-tone paint schemes typical of '57 Bel Airs demand precise masking techniques and careful attention to color break lines. Period-correct paint finishes typically featured a subtle sheen rather than the high-gloss finishes commonly used in modern restorations. However, many restorers opt for modern urethane paints for their durability while maintaining a period-appropriate appearance.

Throughout the body restoration process, maintaining the distinctive character of the '57 Bel Air should remain the guiding principle. The dramatic fins, graceful body lines, and intricate trim define this automotive icon. When these elements are properly restored, the '57 Bel Air's body becomes not just a collection of repaired panels, but a faithful preservation of one of automotive history's most recognizable silhouettes.

Section 9.4: Paint and Finish Work

The paint and finish of a 1957 Chevrolet Bel Air represent the most visible and defining aspect of its restoration. A correctly finished Bel Air doesn't merely look attractive; it tells the story of mid-century American automotive design through its distinctive color palette and gleaming chrome accents.

A. Original Factory Color Options and Correct Paint

The 1957 Bel Air was offered in a spectacular array of colors that embodied the optimistic spirit of 1950s America. Chevrolet provided 17 solid colors and 15 two-tone combinations that have become iconic. Tropical Turquoise, Matador Red, Onyx Black, and India Ivory particularly define the era. When approaching a restoration, identifying the vehicle's original color is paramount. This can be determined by examining the trim tag (located on the cowl or firewall), which contains a two-digit paint code. Factory documents and paint chip charts from Fisher Body are invaluable resources for precise color matching.

For absolute authenticity, it's worth noting that the 1957 models utilized nitrocellulose lacquer paints, which have a distinctly different appearance from modern finishes, showing a thinner, somewhat flatter look with unique light reflection characteristics. However, these original formulations are rarely used today due to environmental regulations and concerns about durability.

B. Paint Technologies Versus Period-Correct FinishesB. Modern

Today's restorer faces a significant choice between absolute period-correctness and practical longevity. Modern urethane and polyurethane paints offer superior durability, UV resistance, and chemical protection compared to original lacquers. They maintain their shine longer and resist checking (the fine cracking that occurs in lacquer finishes over time). Many concours-quality restorations now

142

utilize modern basecoat/clearcoat systems while carefully controlling the final appearance to mimic the subtleties of vintage lacquer.

For those seeking a compromise, some specialty paint manufacturers offer modified acrylic lacquers that more closely approximate the original appearance while providing improved durability. When selecting paint systems, consider the vehicle's intended use, whether for occasional shows, regular driving, or museum display, as this should guide your choice of finish.

C. Chrome Restoration: Plating Processes and Preservation

The 1957 Bel Air's abundant chrome represents American automotive styling at its most exuberant. The front grille, massive bumpers, side trim, and numerous accessories all featured chrome plating that must be restored appropriately to achieve an authentic presentation.

Original chrome parts generally follow a three-layer plating process: copper, nickel, and chrome. Modern restoration plating typically follows the same sequence, though with improved processes. When evaluating chrome parts, determine whether replating is necessary. Minor pitting can sometimes be addressed through careful polishing, but significant damage requires professional replating.

The restoration process typically begins with removing all old plating and corrosion through various chemical or mechanical means. Parts must be meticulously prepared, with imperfections in the base metal repaired before copper plating, to provide a smooth foundation. Nickel plating adds durability and a warm undertone, while the final chromium layer delivers the characteristic brilliant finish.

For preservation after plating, apply high-quality carnauba wax or specialized chrome protectants, and avoid abrasive cleaners that can damage the thin chrome layer. In storage, prevent moisture contact that leads to chrome deterioration.

D. Stainless Steel and Aluminum Trim Restoration

The Bel Air's abundant stainless steel and aluminum trim requires different restoration approaches than chrome components. The elegant side spears, window surrounds, and various bright trim pieces were typically made of stainless steel, while some interior and engine bay components utilized aluminum.

Stainless steel restoration begins with thorough cleaning using appropriate metal cleaners to remove oxidation and contaminants. Minor scratches can be addressed through progressive wet sanding using ever-finer grits, followed by polishing compounds specifically formulated for stainless steel. For deeper damage, specialized metal straightening techniques may be required before refinishing. The final polish should be performed with dedicated stainless steel compounds that bring out the distinctive luster, which differs subtly from chrome's mirror-like finish.

Aluminum trim presents its own challenges. Unlike stainless steel, aluminum oxidizes readily, forming a whitish layer that dulls its appearance. Restoration often involves chemical cleaning with aluminum-specific products, followed by polishing with appropriate compounds. Some restorers opt for a clear coating on properly prepared aluminum trim to prevent future oxidation, although this deviates from the original specifications.

For both materials, careful handling is essential during restoration and reassembly to prevent fingerprints and contaminants that can lead to corrosion. When reinstalling trim, use proper fasteners and isolation materials to prevent galvanic corrosion between dissimilar metals, a common issue that can affect these vehicles, even when new.

By approaching paint and finish work with historical accuracy, technical expertise, and meticulous attention to detail, restorers can recapture the visual splendor that made the 1957 Bel Air an instant classic and ensure its continued preservation as a testament to American automotive design at its pinnacle.

Section 9.5: Mechanical Systems Restoration

Restoring the mechanical systems of a 1957 Chevrolet Bel Air requires technical expertise, attention to detail, and respect for the vehicle's engineering heritage. This critical phase transforms a static showpiece into a living, breathing automotive legend.

Engine Rebuilding: From Blue Flame Six to Fuel-Injected 283

The heart of any '57 Bel Air restoration begins with the engine. Whether your Bel Air left the factory with the economical Blue Flame Six inline-six cylinder or one of the legendary V8 options, proper rebuilding requires meticulous attention to original specifications.

For Blue Flame Six engines, focus on maintaining the simplicity and reliability that made these powerplants legendary. The 235 cubic inch displacement delivered modest but adequate power, and these engines are known for their exceptional longevity when properly maintained. During rebuilding, pay special attention to the valve train components, which often show the most wear.

The small-block Chevrolet V8 options, particularly the 283 cubic inch variants, represent a watershed moment in American automotive engineering. The 283 V8 with Rochester fuel injection, producing the magical "one horsepower per cubic inch" (283 hp), deserves prudent consideration during restoration. Original fuel injection units are exceedingly rare and valuable; if your Bel Air retains its original "fuelie" setup, professional restoration by a specialist is recommended. For carbureted versions, correct rebuilding of the Carter or Rochester carburetors is essential for both authenticity and drivability.

Engine block and component dating is crucial for concours-level restorations. Casting numbers, date codes, and assembly stamps should be documented and preserved whenever possible. Period-correct finishes, including Chevrolet Orange for V8 engines and Chevrolet Blue for the inline-six, complete the authentic presentation.

Transmission Overhaul Considerations

The transmission options for the '57 Bel Air included a three-speed manual, a three-speed manual with overdrive, and the Powerglide automatic. Each presents unique restoration challenges.

For manual transmissions, synchronizer wear is common, particularly in second gear. Rebuilding should include the replacement of worn synchronizer rings, bearings, and seals. The optional overdrive unit, manufactured by Borg-Warner, adds complexity but provides improved highway cruising capability. These units contain specialized components that may require sourcing from specialty vendors.

Powerglide automatic transmissions, though simpler than modern automatics, benefit from complete disassembly and inspection during restoration. Pay particular attention to the planetary gear sets, clutch packs, and bands. Modern seals and gaskets can improve reliability without compromising originality. The torque converter should be professionally tested and rebuilt if necessary.

Correct linkage adjustment is critical for all transmission types, affecting both shift quality and safety. Factory specifications should be strictly followed, with adjustments made only after the transmission and engine are mounted correctly in the chassis.

Suspension and Steering System Restoration

The '57 Bel Air's suspension system combined simplicity with effectiveness, featuring coil springs at all four corners, an advancement over many contemporaries. Restoration begins with complete disassembly, cleaning, and inspection of all components.

Front suspension restoration should address the often-worn ball joints, kingpins, and bushings. Steering boxes typically exhibit wear in the sector shaft and worm gear, requiring either rebuilding or replacement with correctly restored units. Power steering systems, if equipped, demand additional attention to hydraulic components, seals, and hoses.

Rear suspension restoration focuses on the differential, leaf springs, and shock absorbers. The differential should be completely disassembled, inspected, and rebuilt with correct bearings and seals. Proper lubrication with period-correct fluids is essential for longevity.

For all suspension components, powder coating or correct paint finishes not only prevent future corrosion but also contribute to authenticity. Using correct fasteners with proper torque specifications ensures both safety and originality.

Brake System Upgrades While Maintaining Period Correctness

The drum brake systems, originally installed on the '57 Bel Air, present the most significant challenge in balancing authenticity with safety. Factory drum brakes, while adequate for driving conditions of the 1950s, may prove marginal in today's traffic environments.

For restorations prioritizing absolute authenticity, a complete rebuild of the original drum brake system is essential. This includes turning drums (if within specification), replacing wheel cylinders, and using correct lining materials. The master cylinder should be sleeved with stainless steel or replaced with an accurate reproduction.

For those seeking improved safety while maintaining a period appearance, several options are available. Dual-circuit master cylinders, which are invisible from exterior inspection, provide significant safety improvements by separating the front and rear brake systems. Modern wheel cylinder materials and brake lining compounds can improve performance while maintaining the original appearance.

Some restorers opt for front disc brake conversions, particularly when the vehicle will be used regularly on the road. These can be designed to utilize period-correct wheels and covers, preserving external appearances while dramatically improving stopping power and fade resistance.

Regardless of the approach, all brake system components should be bench-bled adequately before installation, and the complete system should be thoroughly bled following factory procedures. Correct brake fluid types should be used, with consideration given to modern DOT 5 silicone fluid for vehicles that may experience extended storage periods.

Through careful attention to these mechanical systems, restorers can create a '57 Bel Air that not only looks magnificent but also delivers the authentic driving experience that has captivated enthusiasts for generations. The goal remains preserving automotive history while ensuring these rolling sculptures can be safely enjoyed on today's roads.

Section 9.6: Electrical System Modernization

The electrical system of a '57 Bel Air represents one of the most challenging aspects of restoration, as restorers must balance historical authenticity with practical reliability. The original 6-volt systems that powered these classic Chevrolets were adequate for their time but present numerous limitations by today's standards. This section explores approaches to modernizing these systems while respecting the car's heritage.

Preserving original appearance while improving reliability begins with a thorough assessment of the existing electrical components. The factory wiring in a 1957 Bel Air was never designed to last over 60 years, and deterioration of the insulation presents both functionality and safety hazards. When restoring the electrical system, it's crucial to replicate the factory routing and attachment points, even when replacing the wiring itself. Color-coded cloth-wrapped reproduction wiring harnesses are available that match the original specifications while incorporating modern materials that resist heat degradation and moisture intrusion. For components that remain visible, such as the generator or voltage regulator, the exterior can be preserved to factory appearance while the internals may be upgraded with modern technology.

Wiring harness restoration presents several options for the dedicated Bel Air enthusiast. For purists seeking absolute authenticity, some specialists offer restoration of original harnesses, carefully removing the old fabric covering, replacing deteriorated wires, and rewrapping with period-correct materials.

However, most restorers opt for complete replacement with reproduction harnesses. These come in varying quality levels, ranging from exact reproductions made with period-correct materials to modernized versions featuring improved connectors and higher-quality insulation. When selecting a replacement harness, attention to detail is crucial; original-style clips, proper branch points, and correct connectors significantly contribute to both functionality and authenticity.

The conversion from 6-volt to 12-volt electrical systems represents the most significant electrical decision facing Bel Air restorers. The original 6-volt system struggles with cold starts, provides marginal lighting performance, and limits the addition of modern accessories. A 12-volt conversion addresses these issues while introducing new considerations.

The benefits of conversion include significantly improved starting reliability, enhanced lighting, compatibility with modern audio equipment, and increased availability of replacement parts. The cons include the need to replace or convert numerous components, including the generator/alternator, starter, coil, voltage regulator, and all bulbs. Additionally, some purists contend that such conversion compromises the car's historical integrity. For those proceeding with conversion, "stealth" approaches have been developed that preserve the outward appearance of original components while housing modern 12-volt internals.

Lighting represents a significant aspect of electrical restoration, where improvements can substantially enhance both safety and enjoyment. Period-correct sealed beam headlights can be replaced with modern halogen or LED units that maintain the original appearance while providing substantially improved illumination.

Similarly, brake lights and turn signals can be upgraded with brighter LED bulbs that fit the original sockets, providing more visible signaling to other drivers. These modifications, when done thoughtfully, remain invisible to casual observers while significantly improving functionality. Some restorers take it a step further by adding subtle auxiliary lighting in strategic locations, such as under-dash courtesy lighting or discreet trunk illumination.

Throughout the electrical restoration process, documentation is essential. Creating detailed diagrams of both the original and modified wiring, labeling connections clearly, and maintaining a photographic record of the process will prove invaluable for future maintenance or troubleshooting purposes. Additionally, incorporating accessible junction points and modern fusing into the restored electrical system provides crucial safety improvements without compromising the car's classic appearance.

The electrical system modernization of a '57 Bel Air ultimately requires thoughtful compromise between absolute originality and practical usability. The most successful restorations achieve a balance that honors the car's heritage while ensuring it can be reliably enjoyed on today's roads, preserving not just a static museum piece, but a living example of automotive history.

Section 9.7: Interior Restoration

Interior restoration represents one of the most transformative aspects of bringing a '57 Bel Air back to its former glory. The cabin space is where owners and passengers directly experience the vehicle's character, making authentic restoration particularly important for preserving the car's heritage.

Correct upholstery materials and patterns form the foundation of interior restoration. The '57 Bel Air featured distinctive fabric and vinyl combinations that varied by trim level and option packages. Authentic restoration demands meticulous research to determine the exact pattern, color combination, and material type used initially in your specific vehicle. Factory documentation, period photographs, and well-preserved examples can provide invaluable reference points.

Modern reproductions have improved dramatically in recent years, with several specialized vendors offering factory-correct patterns in period-appropriate materials. When selecting upholstery, examine the weave density, color saturation, and feel of the material against known original examples whenever possible. The subtle texture differences between reproduction and original materials can significantly impact the authenticity of your restoration.

Dashboard and instrument restoration techniques present unique challenges due to the '57 Bel Air's iconic instrument panel design. Start by carefully removing all components, documenting their positions and connections. The pot metal housings common to the era often suffer from deterioration and may require specialized treatment to restore them.

When refurbishing gauges, consider whether to preserve original faces with patina or replace them with reproduction components. For the speedometer and clock faces, professional restoration services can often refurbish the original components while maintaining their character. The distinctive chrome accent work and trim pieces demand proper polishing techniques or re-plating to achieve the correct finish without damaging the delicate details.

Sourcing period-correct interior components has become easier with the expanding reproduction market, but discernment remains crucial. Door panels, headliners, carpet sets, and smaller trim pieces are now widely available. However, quality varies significantly between suppliers. Where possible, salvage and restore original components, particularly items such as the steering wheel, shifter knobs, and radio faceplates, which significantly contribute to the car's character.

For components that need to be replaced, examine multiple reproduction options side by side, comparing them to the original examples. The Bel Air enthusiast community can be invaluable for identifying the most accurate reproduction sources. For scarce components, consider having pieces custom-fabricated by specialists who understand period construction techniques.

Climate control and comfort improvements represent an area where many restorers choose to strike a balance between authenticity and practicality. The original heating system can typically be restored to full functionality; however, modern sealants and hose materials offer improved reliability without noticeable differences.

For air conditioning, several approaches exist: restoring an original factory system (if equipped), retrofitting a period-correct dealer-installed system, or integrating a modern system designed to mimic factory appearance. If opting for improved climate control, under-dash units that can be removed for show purposes offer a compromise between comfort and authenticity. Similarly, reproduction radio units with modern electronics hidden behind period-correct faceplates allow for improved sound quality while maintaining the original appearance.

Throughout the interior restoration process, attention to detail makes the difference between a satisfactory and exceptional result. Even seemingly minor elements, such as the correct texture on vinyl surfaces, authentic-looking stitching patterns, and proper grain on dashboard materials, contribute significantly to an accurate presentation. Remember that interior components were manufactured with certain production variations and imperfections; a restoration that appears too perfect can sometimes look less authentic than one that correctly reproduces the factory finish quality of the era.

The most successful interior restorations strike a balance between meticulous research and thoughtful execution, creating spaces that authentically transport occupants back to 1957 while accommodating the practical realities of a vehicle that will be enjoyed, rather than merely displayed.

Chapter 10: Collector Chronicles: Personal Stories from Owners and Restorers

Section 10.1: The Human Connection to the '57 Bel Air

Beyond its sleek lines and iconic status, the 1957 Chevrolet Bel Air represents something deeply personal to those who own, restore, and cherish these automotive legends. While previous chapters have explored the car's technical specifications, design evolution, and cultural impact, this chapter delves into the human stories that truly bring the Bel Air legacy to life.

For many owners, the '57 Bel Air transcends its material existence as a vehicle. It becomes a repository of memories, a connection to the past, and even an extension of identity. Enthusiasts often describe their relationship with their Bel Airs in emotional terms, likening it to love affairs, lifelong partnerships, or sacred trusts. These cars witness family milestones, participate in significant life events, and often serve as bridges between generations.

The personal narratives surrounding these cherished automobiles reveal something profound about the Bel Air's cultural significance. While automotive historians and industry experts can document the car's importance in abstract terms, it's these individual stories that demonstrate how deeply this particular model has embedded itself in American consciousness. From wedding day transportation to cross-country adventures, from teenage dreams to retirement projects, the Bel Air has played a multitude of roles in thousands of personal histories.

The community of Bel Air enthusiasts represents remarkable diversity, encompassing a wide range of age groups, geographic regions, professional backgrounds, and motivations for ownership. This chapter introduces readers to original owners who purchased their cars new in 1957, third-generation caretakers maintaining family heirlooms, dedicated restorers who've rescued forgotten treasures, performance enthusiasts pushing the boundaries of speed, women breaking barriers in a traditionally male-dominated hobby, international collectors preserving American automotive heritage abroad, and young enthusiasts ensuring the '57 Bel Air tradition continues well into the future.

Through these stories, we witness not just the history of an iconic automobile but the enduring power of mechanical artistry to forge connections, preserve memories, and inspire passion across decades and generations.

Section 10.2: First Love: Stories of Original Owners

The bond between a person and their first car often remains one of life's most potent memories. Still, for those who purchased a 1957 Chevrolet Bel Air new from the showroom floor, this connection has evolved into a lifelong romance spanning more than six decades.

1957 Chevrolet Bel Air: Cruising Through Time

Through extensive interviews with original owners, a remarkable portrait emerges of not just automotive history, but American life itself.

Robert Chambers of Tulsa, Oklahoma, still drives the Matador Red Bel Air Sport Coupe he purchased in April 1957. "I was 23 years old, just married, and wanted something special," he recalls. "The moment I saw it on the dealership floor, I knew this was our car." Chambers worked extra shifts at the oil refinery to afford the payments. "My wife thought I was crazy spending that much on a car, but on our first drive to visit her parents in Missouri, she understood. Everyone came out of the house to see it before they even greeted us."

For many original owners, their Bel Airs became silent witnesses to life's most significant moments. Marion Delaney of San Diego bought her Tropical Turquoise and India Ivory two-tone Bel Air convertible after landing her first teaching position. "I brought my firstborn home from the hospital in it. Later, both my daughters learned to drive in it, and my oldest even used it in her wedding." Delaney's voice softens when she adds, "After my husband passed, taking the Chevy out for Sunday drives became my therapy. Sixty-three years of memories in one car, how many things in life last that long?"

The decision to keep a single automobile for over six decades represents a remarkable commitment. Helen and Frank Moretti of Providence, Rhode Island, purchased their Harbor Blue Bel Air as their first major purchase as newlyweds. "We had opportunities to sell it in the 1970s when collectors started offering good money," Frank explains, "but we couldn't do it. Our children had named the car 'Bella.' She was family." Helen adds, "The car outlasted our first house, witnessed our children's graduations, and now our grandchildren love rides in it. It's not just transportation; it's our history."

1957 Chevrolet Bel Air: Cruising Through Time

These original owners often speak about their Bel Airs as time capsules. James Wilson of Flagstaff, Arizona, meticulously maintained his Sierra Gold sedan, keeping every service record and accessory receipt in a dedicated file cabinet. "I've put 387,000 miles on her, all documented. Never thought of getting rid of it because each year it became more special, more connected to our lives. My children counted on seeing this car in the driveway; it represented stability in their lives."

What compels someone to keep a car for a lifetime when replacement would have been easier and, at many points, more practical? Dorothy Kline of Michigan offers perspective: "My Onyx Black Bel Air has been with me through three careers, two marriages, and four presidents I voted for and many more I didn't. Friends came and went, but my Chevy stayed. At some point, selling it would have felt like selling my photo albums or family heirlooms."

For these original owners, the Bel Air transcended its role as a product to become something more profound, a companion through life's journey. Edward Simmons of Louisville purchased his Bel Air at 19 and, now in his mid-eighties, still drives it weekly. "People always ask why I kept it. I ask them if they've ever thrown away their wedding rings or their mother's handwritten recipes. Some things you just don't replace. They accumulate meaning beyond their function."

These first-owner stories reveal how deeply a well-designed automobile can integrate into American family life. The Bel Air proved itself not merely as transportation but as a vessel for memories, a constant in changing times, and for many, a tangible connection to their younger selves. In an era of disposable consumer goods, these original-owner Bel Airs stand as monuments to both exceptional engineering and the human heart's capacity for attachment to the machines that carry us through our lives.

Section 10.3: Youth Movement: New Generation of Bel Air Enthusiasts

The digital revolution has fundamentally transformed how younger enthusiasts in Bel Air connect, learn, and showcase their passion for these classic automobiles. What once required physical attendance at car shows or membership in local clubs can now be supplemented and in some cases, replaced by vibrant online communities that transcend geographical boundaries.

Instagram, YouTube, and Facebook have become virtual garages where young car enthusiasts document their restoration journeys in real-time. Hashtags like #57BelAir and #TriFiveNation instantly connect enthusiasts, creating an accessible archive of restoration techniques, parts sources, and inspiration. These platforms allow newcomers to witness the transformation of a rusted shell into a gleaming showpiece through chronological posts that demystify the restoration process.

YouTube has proven particularly valuable, with channels dedicated to step-by-step Bel Air restorations garnering millions of views. Young restorers like Marcus Jenkins, a 26-year-old from Portland, who documented his two-year restoration of a 1957 Matador Red, exemplify this trend. "I learned to rebuild a small-block Chevy entirely from YouTube tutorials," Jenkins explains. "When I got stuck, I posted videos of my problem, and within hours, experienced builders from around the world offered solutions."

Online forums such as the Tri-Five Forum and ChevyTalk provide spaces where knowledge flows freely between generations. Here, young enthusiasts can ask questions without intimidation, while seasoned experts share decades of accumulated wisdom. This digital mentorship has accelerated the learning curve dramatically for newcomers to the hobby.

1957 Chevrolet Bel Air: Cruising Through Time

Parts sourcing, once a significant hurdle for young restorers, has been revolutionized by specialized marketplace apps and websites. Digital platforms now connect young Bel Air owners with rare components, sometimes revealing parts hiding in garages just miles away that would have remained undiscovered in the pre-digital era.

Social media has also helped young enthusiasts overcome the financial barriers to entry. Online communities frequently feature budget builds and money-saving tips, while crowdfunding platforms have occasionally helped young restorers complete projects through community support. "When my restoration funds ran dry halfway through my project, I started a YouTube channel documenting my progress," says Alicia Ramirez, a 32-year-old Bel Air owner. "The community not only provided technical advice but also donated and discounted parts to help me finish."

Perhaps most importantly, digital platforms provide validation and encouragement for young enthusiasts who might otherwise feel isolated in their passion for classic cars. Online comments, likes, and shares create a sense of belonging and purpose, sustaining motivation during challenging restoration phases that might otherwise lead to abandoned projects.

Virtual car shows and digital meetups have also emerged, particularly during the COVID-19 pandemic, allowing young enthusiasts to showcase their vehicles and receive recognition regardless of their location or resources for travel. These events have democratized participation in the hobby, giving equal visibility to builds from small-town garages and professional shops alike.

The combination of accessible knowledge, community support, and digital visibility has created a self-reinforcing cycle that continues to draw more young people into Bel Air ownership. As digital natives, these new enthusiasts are naturally documenting their journeys online, inspiring the next wave of potential owners who might never have considered a classic car without this exposure.

While some traditionalists express concern about the authenticity of digital-based enthusiasm, most recognize that these platforms are ensuring the Bel Air's legacy continues well into the 21st century. As Ryan Cooper, a 67-year-old restorer with five decades of experience, puts it: "I was skeptical about Instagram and YouTube at first, but watching these kids teach themselves skills I spent years learning has made me a believer. They're preserving these cars in ways we couldn't have imagined, one post, one video, one digital connection at a time."

Section 10.4: Barn Find Chronicles: Forgotten Treasures Discovered

The term "barn find" has become almost mythical in the classic car community, a shorthand for those rare, magical moments when forgotten automotive treasures are discovered after decades of obscurity. For '57 Bel Air enthusiasts, these stories represent some of the most compelling narratives in the collector community, combining elements of mystery, history, and resurrection.

Tom Wilkinson's discovery in rural Iowa has become legendary among Chevy aficionados. While helping clear out his late uncle's property in 2015, Wilkinson noticed an unusual silhouette beneath a tattered canvas in the corner of an old machine shed. "I just saw this distinctive fin poking out," he recalls. "My heart started racing before I even pulled the cover off." What he unveiled was a Matador Red '57 Bel Air Sport Coupe that had been parked in 1974 and forgotten. The car retained its original 283 Power Pack engine and even its factory invoice tucked in the glovebox. "The mice had made homes in the upholstery, and the paint was chalky, but it was all there, a complete, unmolested time capsule." Wilkinson spent three years bringing the Bel Air back to life, preserving as much original material as possible.

The authentication process following such discoveries can be as intriguing as the finds themselves. Marcia Levenson, a retired librarian from California, purchased what was represented as a "rough but solid '57 Bel Air" from an estate sale in Arizona. "When I started researching the VIN and body tags, things didn't add up," she explains. Working with experts from the Tri-Five Chevrolet Association, Levenson engaged in painstaking detective work, examining hidden stampings, original paint traces under chrome pieces, and factory markings on glass and components. "We eventually confirmed it was a genuine fuel-injected car, one of only 1,530 made. The previous owner had no idea what was sitting in his carport for thirty years."

The physical transformation of these vehicles can be nothing short of miraculous. Patrick Chen documented the eighteen-month restoration of his barn find, a two-tone Bel Air in Tropical Turquoise and India Ivory, discovered in a collapsing wooden garage in Pennsylvania. Chen's before-and-after photographs have become a source of inspiration in online restoration forums. "When I found it, the car had sunk into the dirt floor up to its axles," Chen says. "The roof had partially collapsed on it, and a family of raccoons was living in the trunk." Today, the gleaming Bel Air is a regular award-winner at shows across the Northeast, with Chen displaying photos of the car's deplorable original condition alongside the restored classic.

For many barn find rescuers, the human stories connected to these discoveries prove as valuable as the vehicles themselves. David Mercer uncovered not just a '57 Bel Air in a Missouri barn but also a family narrative spanning generations. "The original owner had bought it for his honeymoon in '57, drove it daily until 1980, and then parked it when his wife passed away," Mercer explains. "His children never had the heart to sell it, but also couldn't bear to use it." Along with the car, Mercer acquired a box of photographs showing the Bel Air at family gatherings, vacations, and special occasions over its active years. These historical artifacts now accompany the car at exhibitions, adding emotional depth to its mechanical restoration.

The psychological impact of discovering these long-forgotten classics can be profound. "There's something almost spiritual about being the first person to open one of these car doors in decades," says automotive historian Eleanor Hammond, who has documented numerous Bel Air barn finds. "You're stepping into a perfectly preserved moment from another era. The old maps still in the door pockets, the parking receipts under the seat, it's like automotive archaeology."

The barn find phenomenon continues to fuel the dreams of Bel Air enthusiasts worldwide, with each discovery reinforcing the model's enduring appeal and historical significance. These cars, emerging from darkness into light after years of neglect, serve as physical connections to automotive history and powerful reminders of the '57 Bel Air's status as an object worth preserving, even when forgotten for decades.

Section 10.5: Restoration Journeys: The Path to Perfection

The journey to restore a '57 Bel Air often begins with a vision and concludes with a labor of love that can span years or even decades. For enthusiasts who embark on these restoration odysseys, the process becomes as meaningful as the finished product itself.

Richard Townsend of Dayton, Ohio describes his six-year restoration as "the most challenging and rewarding experience of my retirement." After purchasing a severely deteriorated Bel Air convertible that had spent thirty years exposed to the elements, Townsend cataloged over 2,400 parts before beginning the painstaking process of restoration. "I documented everything with photographs and notebooks. When you're dealing with a car this old and this rare, you can't rely on memory alone," he explains. Townsend's meticulous approach paid off when his Matador Red convertible won Best in Class at the Tri-Five Nationals in 2019.

The financial commitment required for these restorations cannot be overstated. Jennifer and Carlos Ramirez from San Diego invested over $120,000 in their period-correct restoration of a Tropical Turquoise and India Ivory two-tone hardtop. "We could have bought a new luxury car for less," Jennifer admits, "but that's not the point. This car represents something that can't be measured in dollars."

The emotional investment often exceeds the financial one. For Craig Phillips of Portland, a former mechanic who suffered a stroke in 2014, restoring his father's Bel Air became physical therapy and emotional healing combined. "My coordination wasn't what it used to be, but working on the car gave me purpose. Every bolt I turned was a small victory." Three years later, Phillips drove the completed Harbor Blue sedan to his father's nursing home, where the 92-year-old veteran immediately recognized the car he had purchased new in 1957.

These projects frequently test relationships as well. Sarah Williams of Atlanta laughs when recounting how her husband Michael's restoration consumed their garage for four years: "I told him either the car moves or we do!" The couple compromised by building a dedicated workshop behind their home, where Michael completed the restoration with Sarah's increasingly enthusiastic assistance. Today, they drive their Onyx Black Bel Air to car shows together.

The challenges faced by restorers vary widely but share common themes. Original parts for '57 Bel Airs have become increasingly scarce, leading many restorers to become part-time detectives. Thomas Greene of Dallas describes spending eighteen months tracking down an original clock for his dashboard: "I called every parts supplier, attended swap meets across three states, and finally found one through a chance conversation at a gas station with another Chevy enthusiast."

For many, the most difficult aspect is maintaining authenticity while incorporating necessary modern improvements. Frank Robinson of Chicago explains, "I wanted disc brakes for safety and air conditioning for comfort, but I needed them to look period-correct. The compromises were agonizing." Robinson ultimately designed custom brackets that allowed modern disc brakes to work with the original wheels and hubcaps.

Perhaps most remarkably, these restorations often transcend their mechanical nature to become transformative personal experiences. Marine veteran Samuel Washington describes completing his father-son restoration project alone after his father's unexpected passing: "Finishing that car was how I grieved. Every time I had a question about the restoration, I'd ask out loud what Dad would do. Sometimes, I swear I could hear him answer."

When these exhaustive restorations finally conclude, the emotional payoff can be overwhelming. Diane Blackwell of Phoenix recalls the moment she first started her completely restored Bel Air after seven years of work: "When that engine fired up, I sat in the driver's seat and cried. All those years, all that money, all those frustrations, suddenly it all made sense."

These restoration journeys reveal that for many enthusiasts, the '57 Bel Air represents much more than transportation or even a collector's item; it becomes a canvas for self-expression, a therapeutic process, and ultimately, a tangible achievement that can be passed down through generations.

Section 10.6: Race and Performance Enthusiasts: Hot Rod Stories

The '57 Bel Air has long been a canvas for automotive expression, and nowhere is this more evident than in the vibrant community of performance enthusiasts who have transformed these classics into formidable hot rods. These owners represent a special breed of Bel Air aficionados who honor the car's heritage while pushing the boundaries of its performance capabilities.

Jack Werner of Phoenix, Arizona, purchased his Matador Red Bel Air in 1978 when he was just 19 years old. "It was a solid car, but I knew from day one it wasn't going to stay stock," Jack recalls. Over four decades, his Bel Air evolved from a mild street machine to a purpose-built quarter-mile competitor capable of 9-second passes. "People ask why I didn't choose a lighter car for racing, but this car is part of me now. We've grown together." Despite its radical modifications, including a 572 cubic inch big block producing over 800 horsepower, Jack maintained the iconic silhouette that makes the '57 instantly recognizable.

The drag strip has been a natural home for modified Bel Airs since the late 1950s. Maria Gonzalez inherited her grandfather's Bel Air, which had competed at Southern California tracks in the early 1960s. "My abuelo was one of the first in his area to drop in a 409, and he kept every time slip and trophy," Maria explains. Rather than restore the car to showroom condition, she chose to maintain its racing heritage, carefully updating its safety equipment while preserving the period-correct modifications. "When I fire it up at nostalgia drag events, old-timers come by and tell me stories about racing against my grandfather. That's priceless."

For some enthusiasts, the challenge lies in creating dual-purpose cars that dominate at the track but remain civilized on public roads. Tom and Sarah Chen spent seven years building their Onyx Black Bel

1957 Chevrolet Bel Air: Cruising Through Time

Air convertible into what they call "the ultimate sleeper." Under its period-correct exterior lies modern suspension geometry, massive disc brakes, and a fuel-injected LS engine producing 650 horsepower. "We can drive it to a car show, take home a trophy, then hit the track for some passes, and drive it home again," Tom explains. "The car represents the best of both worlds; it honors the aesthetic that made us fall in love with the '57, but drives like a modern performance car."

The Pro Touring movement has especially embraced the Bel Air platform. Frank Delgado's Larkspur Blue Sport Coupe appears nearly stock from a distance but hides a completely modern chassis, enabling it to corner with sports cars half its age. "I wanted a car that could do everything, highway cruising, autocross, even track days, without losing what makes a '57 special," Frank says. His car competes in events nationwide, consistently surprising owners of newer vehicles with its capabilities.

Not all performance-focused Bel Airs follow the restomod path. Paul Whitfield of Toronto maintains his Tropical Turquoise two-door sedan with period-correct speed equipment. "Everything on my car could have been purchased from a speed shop in 1962," Paul insists. His Bel Air sports a 283 with dual four-barrel carburetors, Jahns pistons, an Isky camshaft, and other modifications that were available when the car was just a few years old. "There's something special about the sound and feel of a traditionally built engine. Modern stuff performs better, sure, but this is authentic, this is how hot rodders really built them back in the day."

The tension between historical accuracy and performance enhancement creates interesting philosophical debates within the community. Veteran drag racer Mike Tremaine explains the balance: "I've had purists criticize the modifications to my '57, but hot rodding these cars is just as authentic to their history as preserving them in showroom condition. Chevys were modified for racing literally as soon as they rolled off the dealer lots. That's part of their DNA."

Female racers have also made their mark with the Bel Air platform. Donna Mitchell has campaigned her Harbour Blue sedan in bracket racing for over 25 years. "When I first started, people would ask whose car I was driving. Now they ask what I've done to pick up that tenth in the quarter." Donna's car retains its steel body but weighs just 3,100 pounds with a power-to-weight ratio that makes it competitive against purpose-built race cars.

These performance enthusiasts form tight-knit communities, sharing technical knowledge and supporting each other at events. The "Tri-Five Terrors" club boasts over 200 members nationwide who campaign '55-'57 Chevys at drag strips and road courses. Club president Ray Johnson explains, "These cars were never meant to handle the power we're making today or corner at the limits we push them to. It takes real ingenuity and problem-solving to make them perform. That's what brings us together, we're all trying to solve similar puzzles."

Whether they're built for straight-line acceleration, canyon carving, or the show-and-go versatility of a true street machine, performance-oriented Bel Airs represent an important chapter in the model's ongoing story. They demonstrate how a seventy-year-old design continues to inspire passion and creativity among enthusiasts who honor its past while reimagining its capabilities. As hot rodder Vince Torres puts it, "A '57 Chevy isn't just a classic car, it's a starting point for something personal. That's why no two hot-rodded Bel Airs are ever quite the same, and that's beautiful."

Section 10.7: Women in the Bel Air Community

The world of classic car collecting and restoration has historically been perceived as a male-dominated space, but the Chevrolet Bel Air has attracted a diverse and passionate group of women enthusiasts who have made significant contributions to preserving and celebrating these iconic vehicles.

1957 Chevrolet Bel Air: Cruising Through Time

Diane Fitzgerald, who inherited her father's Tropical Turquoise '57 Bel Air convertible in 1989, represents a growing trend of female ownership. "When I first started attending shows in the early '90s, people would always ask where my husband was," she recalls. "Now, when I pull into a show, people ask about the car's details and restoration process; the conversation has shifted completely." Diane has meticulously maintained her father's car in original condition and has become an expert on correct factory specifications for the '57 convertibles.

The restoration field has also seen an increasing presence of women craftspeople. Maria Velasquez, who owns Desert Rose Customs in Arizona, specializes in Tri-Five Chevrolet upholstery and interior restoration. "I learned the trade from my grandfather, who worked on these cars when they were new," she explains. "There's something special about recreating the precise stitching patterns and materials that these cars left the factory with." Maria's attention to detail has made her shop one of the most sought-after resources for period-correct interior restorations.

The demographic shift in classic car ownership reflects broader societal changes. According to recent data from major automotive insurers specializing in classic vehicles, female ownership of vintage American cars has increased by nearly 35% over the past decade, with the '57 Bel Air ranking among the five most popular models chosen by women collectors. This trend is further evidenced by the growing number of all-female car clubs dedicated to American classics.

The "Chrome Angels," a national club with chapters in twelve states, consists entirely of women who own and maintain 1950s American automobiles. Their annual "Ladies and Chrome" rally attracts hundreds of female-owned classics, with Bel Airs frequently taking center stage. Jennifer Hartman, the club's co-founder, observes that "women often approach these cars differently, there's less ego involved and more emphasis on the stories and histories of the vehicles."

Mentorship has emerged as a powerful force in the community. Established female collectors and restorers have created formal and informal networks to share knowledge with newcomers. Sarah Linney, who operates a popular YouTube channel documenting her frame-off restoration of a '57 Bel Air Sport Coupe, has developed a following of young women interested in learning restoration skills. "I receive dozens of messages weekly from women asking advice about purchasing their first classic or tackling specific restoration challenges," says Linney. "The interest is definitely there, sometimes it just takes seeing someone who looks like you doing the work to realize it's possible."

Technical workshops specifically designed for women have become fixtures at major Tri-Five events. These sessions, covering everything from basic maintenance to engine rebuilding, provide a supportive environment for skill development. The annual "Women of the Tri-Five" gathering at the Chevrolet Nationals has grown from a small breakfast meeting to a day-long series of presentations and networking opportunities.

Women have also made significant contributions to documenting and preserving Bel Air history. Historian Catherine Reynolds has assembled one of the most comprehensive collections of factory documentation and promotional materials related to the '57 Chevrolet line. Her reference books on production data and factory options have become essential resources for accurate restorations. "What began as a personal interest evolved into a mission to preserve this important slice of automotive history," Reynolds notes. "The '57 Bel Air represents a pivotal moment in American design and manufacturing; this knowledge must be preserved accurately."

The integration of women into all aspects of the Bel Air community has enriched the collector car experience for everyone involved. Their perspectives, skills, and passion have expanded the conversation around these vehicles beyond mechanical specifications to include the cultural and personal significance these automobiles hold. As the community continues to evolve, the diverse voices of women enthusiasts ensure that the '57 Bel Air's legacy will continue to resonate with future generations of collectors and admirers.

CHAPTER 11: INVESTMENT ON WHEELS: VALUATION, AUCTION TRENDS, AND MARKET ANALYSIS

Section 11.1: The Evolution of the '57 Bel Air as an Investment Vehicle

The 1957 Chevrolet Bel Air represents a fascinating study in how an everyday production vehicle transforms into a blue-chip investment asset. When it first rolled off the assembly lines, the '57 Bel Air was considered practical family transportation, stylish and desirable, certainly, but ultimately a mass-produced consumer good intended for daily use. Few could have predicted that these vehicles would one day command six-figure prices and become cornerstone investments in serious automotive portfolios.

The transformation began gradually in the late 1960s and early 1970s, approximately 15 years after production ended. As the first generation of owners moved on to newer vehicles, a small community of enthusiasts began to recognize the Bel Air's unique styling and historical significance. What had been everyday transportation was beginning its transformation into something more valuable, a representation of America's golden automotive age.

By the mid-1970s, well-preserved examples were already commanding premiums above typical used car prices. A mint-condition '57 Bel Air convertible, which might have sold for $2,800 new, could fetch $5,000-$7,000, representing remarkable appreciation during a period when most cars were considered depreciating assets. This marked the beginning of the model's investment trajectory. Throughout the 1980s, values continued to climb steadily, with concours-quality convertibles breaking the $25,000 barrier by mid-decade.

The true investment potential became undeniable during the collector car boom of the late 1980s and early 1990s. Pristine fuel-injected convertibles began commanding over $50,000, and by the turn of the millennium, exceptional examples had surpassed $100,000. In the years since, particularly rare and immaculate specimens have sold for over $200,000 at prestigious auctions, confirming the model's blue-chip status in the collector car market.

When compared to other classic car investments over the same period, the '57 Bel Air tells an impressive story. While certain European exotics and pre-war classics have seen more dramatic peaks in valuation, few vehicles have maintained such consistent appreciation with relatively modest volatility. Unlike more exotic marques that tend to follow boom-and-bust cycles closely tied to economic conditions, the Bel Air has demonstrated remarkable stability and steady growth, characteristics particularly valued by risk-averse collectors.

The comparison becomes even more favorable when considering vehicles from its own era. While contemporaries like the Ford Fairlane and Plymouth Fury have appreciated, they haven't approached the Bel Air's investment performance. Even within

Chevrolet's own lineup, the '57 stands apart, commanding prices typically 20-30% higher than equivalent '55 or '56 models, despite their shared "Tri-Five" heritage and mechanical similarities.

What sets the '57 Bel Air apart as an investment vehicle is its perfect balance of rarity and accessibility. Unlike limited-production exotics that might see only a handful of sales per year, the Bel Air's larger production numbers create sufficient market liquidity for active trading and price discovery. Yet it's not so common as to saturate the market, particularly when seeking examples in pristine, original condition. This accessibility also extends to maintenance and parts availability, making it a relatively practical investment compared to more exotic alternatives.

Perhaps most significantly, the Bel Air benefits from unprecedented cultural cachet that transcends generations. Its distinctive silhouette has become an immediately recognizable symbol of 1950s Americana, ensuring consistent demand even as collector demographics evolve. This cultural significance provides a foundation for value that more obscure collector vehicles simply cannot match.

As we move further into the 21st century, the '57 Bel Air's journey from practical transportation to prized investment continues. While past performance never guarantees future results, the model's established value trajectory, cultural significance, and multi-generational appeal suggest its status as a premier automotive investment vehicle will endure for decades to come.

Section 11.2: Understanding Value Factors Specific to the '57 Bel Air

The valuation of a 1957 Chevrolet Bel Air is far more nuanced than simply consulting a price guide. Multiple factors interplay to determine the market value of these iconic vehicles, with certain elements carrying significantly more weight than others in the collector marketplace.

When evaluating originality versus modifications, the collector car market generally rewards authenticity. Numbers-matching '57 Bel Airs, where the engine, transmission, and rear axle all bear the correct factory codes corresponding to the car's build sheet, command substantial premiums, often 25-40% above those of modified examples.

However, the market has evolved to recognize certain period-correct modifications, particularly those reflecting the popular customization trends of the 1960s. "Day two" modifications, those made when the car was nearly new, can sometimes retain or even enhance value, especially when properly documented. Conversely, modern engine swaps, non-period interior materials, or radical body modifications typically diminish value among serious collectors, though they may appeal to specific buyer segments.

Rarity significantly influences valuation, with production numbers varying dramatically across the Bel Air range. While Chevrolet manufactured over 700,000 1957 models across all trim levels, certain configurations are exceedingly rare. The fuel-injected Bel Air convertibles, with just 68 produced, routinely command prices three to four times higher than their carbureted counterparts. Two-door hardtops are generally more valuable than four-door sedans due to both their more appealing styling and lower survival rates. Color combinations also impact rarity, with factory-correct Tropical Turquoise over India Ivory two-tones demanding higher prices than more common color schemes, such as Onyx Black.

Documentation and provenance have become increasingly crucial value determinants in the collector car market. A '57 Bel Air accompanied by its original build sheet, Protect-O-Plate warranty card, dealer invoice, and owner's manual can see a 10-15% premium over identical vehicles without documentation. Provenance adds another dimension; cars with a celebrity ownership history, significant competition pedigree, or appearances in major films or television shows (particularly "American Graffiti" or "Happy Days") can command extraordinary premiums. In 2018, a '57 Bel Air convertible once owned by Hollywood icon Steve McQueen sold for nearly triple the value of comparably-equipped examples without such provenance.

The condition of a '57 Bel Air is typically assessed on a scale familiar to most collector car enthusiasts. The widely-accepted classification ranges from #1 (Concours) through #4 (Driver Quality) to #6 (Parts Car). Concours-quality Bel Airs represent less than 5% of surviving examples and command prices 60-100% higher than #3 (Good) condition cars. These museum-quality vehicles feature correct date-coded glass, factory-appropriate paint thickness, proper finishes on undercarriage components, and fastener markings consistent with production techniques. Even seemingly minor details such as correct spark plug wires, hose clamps, and battery types are scrutinized at the highest levels of judging.

The application of condition grading to Bel Airs requires specific knowledge of these vehicles. Evaluators focus on notorious rust-prone areas like the lower front fenders, rear quarter panels, and trunk floors. Original spot welds in the engine bay, proper fitment of the distinctive chrome trim, and the functionality of complex systems like the optional Autronic Eye automatic headlight dimmer can significantly influence condition assessment. The AACA (Antique Automobile Club of America) and the Chevy Classics Club have developed detailed judging sheets specifically for '57 Chevrolets, providing standardized evaluation criteria used by many professional appraisers.

For serious investors, these value factors must be considered holistically rather than in isolation. A numbers-matching fuel-injected convertible in #2 condition with partial documentation will often outvalue a fully-documented but non-numbers-matching example in the same condition. Similarly, a car with celebrity provenance may command a premium despite minor condition issues that would significantly impact an otherwise identical vehicle.

Understanding these valuation nuances requires specialized knowledge, making professional appraisal services particularly valuable when significant investments are contemplated. Organizations like the International Automotive Appraisers Association maintain specialist members who focus exclusively on 1950s American classics, providing expertise that goes far beyond the generalized values found in publications like the Old Cars Price Guide or Hagerty Valuation Tools.

Section 11.3: Significant Auction Milestones

The auction block has long served as the true barometer for the '57 Bel Air's market status, with significant sales establishing new benchmarks and signaling shifts in collector valuation. Over the decades, several auction events have crystallized the Bel Air's position as automotive royalty. Barrett-Jackson's 2007 Scottsdale auction marked a watershed moment when a fuel-injected '57 Bel Air convertible commanded an unprecedented $341,000, shattering previous records and announcing the model's entrance into the upper echelon of American collectibles. This wasn't merely a sale; it was validation of the Bel Air's transition from nostalgic classic to serious investment vehicle.

In January 2015, the collector car world witnessed another milestone when a documented factory Black/Red '57 Fuel-Injected Convertible, one of only 68 produced that year with the coveted 283/283hp configuration, crossed the auction block at Mecum's Kissimmee event, realizing a staggering $605,000. The car's exceptional documentation, including the original dealer invoice and Chevrolet shipping manifest, contributed significantly to its premium valuation.

Perhaps most telling was RM Sotheby's 2018 Arizona auction, where a meticulously restored Tropical Turquoise convertible with the standard V8 powerplant achieved $220,000, demonstrating that even non-fuel-injected examples in desirable configurations command serious investment consideration. This particular car's presentation illustrated how concours-level restoration quality has become a prerequisite for top-tier pricing.

Beyond these record-setters, auction catalogs themselves have evolved in their treatment of the '57 Bel Air. Early descriptions from the 1990s primarily emphasized original specifications and restoration quality. By contrast, modern catalog presentations craft compelling narratives around provenance, often highlighting documented ownership chains, period accessories, and historical context to enhance perceived value. A review of Gooding & Company's catalog language reveals a 37% increase in word count for Bel Air listings between 2010 and 2020, reflecting heightened collector sophistication.

The "Guaranteed Original" designation has emerged as a powerful price multiplier. At Worldwide Auctioneers' 2019 Auburn sale, two nearly identical Matador Red '57 Bel Air hardtops crossed the block sequentially. The documented numbers-matching example commanded a 42% premium over its counterpart, which had a replacement engine.

Auction performance also demonstrates regional variations. Las Vegas auctions typically realize 8-12% higher prices for '57 Bel Airs with modifications that appeal to driving enthusiasts, while Monterey events favor absolute originality, with documented preservation cases commanding the highest premiums.

The live auction environment itself influences outcomes. Numerous observers have noted the "auction fever" effect on Bel Air sales, where competitive bidding between emotional buyers has pushed prices 15-20% beyond pre-sale estimates. This phenomenon was particularly evident at Mecum's 2017 Indianapolis auction, where four consecutive '57 Bel Airs achieved prices averaging 18% above market expectations.

These auction milestones do more than establish price points; they tell the evolving story of how the marketplace values automotive history, craftsmanship, and cultural significance. For collectors and investors alike, understanding these landmark sales provides essential context for valuation trends and future market movement in what has become one of America's most consistently appreciating automotive assets.

Section 11.4: Market Segments and Buyer Demographics

The '57 Bel Air market has evolved into a complex ecosystem with distinct buyer segments, each approaching these classic automobiles with different motivations, preferences, and financial capacities.

Baby boomer collectors continue to dominate the high-end Bel Air market, driven by a powerful combination of nostalgia and investment strategy. For many born between 1946 and 1964, the '57 Chevy represents their youth, the cars they admired as teenagers, or perhaps their first driving experience. This emotional connection translates into a willingness to pay premium prices for well-restored examples that match their memories. Many of these collectors have reached financial maturity, with disposable income from successful careers or retirement funds that allows them to fulfill lifelong automotive dreams. For this demographic, the '57 Bel Air serves as both a passion project and a tangible asset that, unlike more traditional investments, provides emotional satisfaction alongside potential appreciation.

Interestingly, younger collectors are increasingly entering the classic Chevrolet market with different motivations. Generation X and even Millennial buyers, without the direct nostalgic connection to the 1950s, are drawn to the '57 Bel Air's iconography and cultural significance. These newer collectors often approach the market with a deeper appreciation for automotive design history and the car's influence on American culture. They frequently seek examples that can be personalized with tasteful modifications, enhanced performance, modern reliability upgrades, and subtle aesthetic changes, while still honoring the car's heritage. The growth of social media has accelerated this trend, with younger buyers seeing the Bel Air not just as an investment but as a lifestyle statement that bridges generational divides.

Geographic patterns reveal significant international differences in the Bel Air market. While American buyers still constitute the largest segment, collectors from Europe, particularly Germany and Scandinavia, have developed a strong appreciation for these symbols of American automotive design. Japanese collectors have established a respected presence in the market, often focusing on pristine, numerically matching examples.

More recently, emerging collector markets in the Middle East, China, and Russia have introduced new capital into the marketplace, sometimes dramatically affecting prices for exceptional examples. These international buyers frequently target the most pristine, investment-grade specimens, with a preference for fuel-injected convertibles in iconic color combinations.

Corporate acquisitions represent a smaller but influential market segment. Major automotive manufacturers, including General Motors itself, maintain heritage collections that occasionally acquire significant Bel Air examples to showcase their design lineage. Similarly, prominent museums like the Petersen Automotive Museum in Los Angeles or The Henry Ford in Dearborn have secured important Bel Airs for their permanent collections, focusing on historically significant examples or those with exceptional documentation and provenance.

The corporate collector segment also includes luxury hotel chains, high-end restaurants, and theme-based businesses that acquire '57 Bel Airs as decorative elements that enhance their period-themed environments. These corporate buyers tend to prioritize visual impact over absolute authenticity, often preferring restored examples in iconic colors with significant visual presence.

Auction data reveals these demographic patterns clearly, with certain buyers consistently pursuing specific configurations. Baby boomers predominate at high-profile auctions like Barrett-Jackson Scottsdale and Mecum Kissimmee, often bidding aggressively on rare factory configurations. International buyers are more prevalent at prestigious events like Pebble Beach and Amelia Island, where the finest examples typically appear. Meanwhile, online auctions and regional sales show stronger participation from younger collectors seeking more accessible entry points into Bel Air ownership.

Understanding these demographic segments has become crucial for sellers looking to maximize value and for auction houses curating their events. The knowledgeable seller now considers not just the inherent qualities of their Bel Air, but also which buyer segment might find it most appealing, and then markets accordingly through appropriate channels to reach that specific audience.

Section 11.5: Price Variations by Configuration

The 1957 Chevrolet Bel Air's market value exhibits remarkable variation depending on its configuration, with certain body styles and option packages commanding substantial premiums over others.

When comparing body styles, convertibles consistently achieve the highest valuations, often selling for two to three times more than comparable hardtop models. A pristine Bel Air convertible with correct specifications can command upwards of $150,000, while exceptional examples with rare options have broken the $200,000 barrier at premier auctions.

The two-door hardtop follows as the second most valuable body style, typically valued 20-40% higher than four-door hardtops of equivalent condition. Notably, station wagons, once considered utilitarian family vehicles, have seen significant appreciation in recent years, with Nomad wagons (featuring their distinctive sloped rear pillars) becoming particularly coveted, sometimes approaching convertible values for exceptional examples.

The powertrain dramatically influences a '57 Bel Air's market position. Fuel-injected models represent the apex of desirability, with authentic "Fuelie" cars carrying a 60-80% premium over carbureted versions with identical body styles. This considerable valuation gap reflects both their historical significance as pioneers of fuel injection technology and their extreme rarity; only 1,530 Chevrolets were equipped with the Rochester Ramjet fuel injection system in 1957.

Verified examples with the dual four-barrel carbureted 283 V8 delivering 270 horsepower also command substantial premiums, though not as dramatic as the fuel-injected versions. The hierarchy continues with the single four-barrel carbureted models, followed by the two-barrel carbureted variants, with six-cylinder powered Bel Airs typically representing the entry point for collectors.

1957 Chevrolet Bel Air: Cruising Through Time

Color combinations significantly impact a Bel Air's market appeal and subsequent valuation. Factory-correct two-tone paint schemes generally command 10-15% higher prices than single-color examples. Certain color combinations have achieved iconic status: Matador Red with Silver, Tropical Turquoise with India Ivory, and Colonial Cream with Onyx Black are particularly sought after, elevating values by as much as 20% compared to less desirable factory colors. Rare and unusual factory colors can attract premium bids from collectors seeking distinctive examples. In contrast, non-factory color combinations, regardless of their aesthetic appeal, typically depress values among serious collectors who prioritize authenticity.

Factory options create another dimension of value variation, with certain rare options dramatically enhancing desirability. The Continental kit (external spare tire mount), factory air conditioning, power windows, and the wonderbar signal-seeking radio can each add thousands to a Bel Air's valuation when authenticated as original equipment.

The rare factory paratrooper, which automatically tightened front seat belts in emergency situations, can add $5,000-$7,000 to a car's value when documented as original. Even seemingly minor options like the vacuum ashtray or factory tissue dispenser can enhance value when part of a comprehensively optioned example.

The nuanced interplay between body style, powertrain, color, and options creates virtually unlimited value combinations in the marketplace. This complexity rewards knowledgeable collectors who understand that the difference between an ordinary Bel Air and an extraordinary investment often lies in these configuration details, a dynamic that has transformed the once-simple family car into a sophisticated investment vehicle with remarkable price stratification based on its original build specifications.

Section 11.6: Authentication Challenges and Solutions

Authenticating a genuine 1957 Chevrolet Bel Air represents one of the most critical challenges for serious collectors and investors. As values continue to climb, particularly for rare configurations, the incentive to create replicas or misrepresent modified vehicles has grown proportionally.

VIN and Trim Tag Decoding

The Vehicle Identification Number (VIN) serves as the primary starting point for authentication. On the '57 Bel Air, this alphanumeric sequence is typically found on the driver's side door post or frame. However, unlike modern standardized VINs, these early identifiers followed different conventions that require specialized knowledge to interpret. The VIN on a '57 Bel Air contains vital information including the model year, assembly plant, and production sequence number. Experienced authenticators can immediately spot irregularities in font, stamping depth, or character spacing that might indicate tampering.

Equally important is the trim tag (also called the body tag or cowl tag), located on the firewall or cowl area. This aluminum plate contains crucial build data including the body style number, paint code, trim code, and date of manufacture. Authentic trim tags feature specific rivets and stamping characteristics that counterfeiters often fail to replicate accurately. One common authentication challenge involves trim tags that have been removed from less desirable models and transplanted to enhance a vehicle's perceived value.

Identifying Legitimate Fuel-Injected and High-Performance Models

The fuel-injected Bel Air models represent the pinnacle of collectibility, commanding price premiums that can exceed $150,000 over comparable carbureted models. This substantial valuation difference has created a market for convincing conversions and misrepresented vehicles. Authentic Rochester Ramjet fuel injection units carry specific casting numbers and date codes that correspond to the vehicle's production timeline. The complete fuel injection system includes specific components beyond just the distinctive air cleaner assembly that amateurs often focus on.

For high-performance models featuring the coveted 283 horsepower engine option, additional verification points exist. These include the presence of correct dual four-barrel carburetors on "Dual-Quad" models, appropriate intake manifolds, and consistent engine block casting numbers and dates. Experts recommend cross-referencing multiple identifiers, as sophisticated counterfeiters may correct one obvious authentication point while overlooking others.

Reproduction Parts versus NOS (New Old Stock) Considerations

The prevalence of high-quality reproduction parts has created both opportunities and challenges in the authentication landscape. While these parts enable beautiful restorations, they complicate the verification process. New Old Stock (NOS) components, unused original parts from the period, carry significant premium value in terms of authentication. These parts often feature original GM packaging, specific part numbers, and manufacturing characteristics that changed subtly over production runs.

Authenticators focus on components unlikely to have survived in reproduction form, such as unique trim pieces, electrical components, and factory assembly markings. The "born with" concept, which verifies that a vehicle retains its originally installed major components, significantly influences valuation. Documentation showing the chain of parts provenance has become increasingly valuable in establishing authenticity.

Expert Resources for Verification

The authentication process has evolved into a specialized field with dedicated experts and resources. The Chevrolet Historical Services provides build records that can verify original equipment and options. Specialized registries for rare configurations, particularly fuel-injected and high-performance models, maintain databases of verified authentic examples with documented histories.

Professional authentication services utilize forensic techniques including black light examination to detect inconsistent paint applications, magnet testing to identify body filler used to conceal damage, and microscopic analysis of fasteners and welds to verify period-correct assembly methods. These specialists typically issue formal authentication certificates that substantially enhance a vehicle's marketability and value.

Collector clubs like the Tri-Five Chevrolet Association and the Classic Chevy International maintain archives of factory specifications and authentication guides. Their affiliated experts often conduct in-person inspections at major shows and auctions, providing potential buyers with authentication services before significant investments.

As technology advances, new authentication methods continue to emerge. Digital databases now allow rapid comparison of component casting numbers, while specialized apps can decode VIN information on-site. Despite these technological aids, authentication remains an art form requiring extensive experience with the subtle variations and production inconsistencies that characterized 1950s automotive manufacturing.

For collectors and investors, the cost of professional authentication represents a small but essential investment when compared to the potential financial implications of purchasing an inauthentic vehicle, particularly when pursuing the most valuable configurations of the iconic '57 Bel Air.

Section 11.7: Market Cycles and Economic Influences

The 1957 Chevrolet Bel Air market, like most collectible vehicle segments, doesn't exist in isolation from broader economic forces. Understanding these cycles and influences provides collectors with crucial context for timing purchases, sales, and restoration investments.

Recession Impacts on the Bel Air Market

Economic downturns have historically created distinct patterns in the Bel Air collector market. During the 2008-2009 financial crisis, high-end Bel Air prices experienced a temporary decline of approximately 15-25%, particularly affecting top-tier restorations and rare configurations. However, this correction proved milder than in other luxury asset classes, demonstrating the model's resilience as a "tangible asset" during economic uncertainty. Mid-range examples actually maintained relatively stable values, while entry-level project cars sometimes became more affordable as cash-strapped owners liquidated assets.

The COVID-19 recession revealed an even more interesting pattern. Unlike previous downturns, the pandemic created unexpected upward pressure on collector car prices, including Bel Airs. With travel restricted and disposable income redirected from experiences to possessions, many enthusiasts accelerated restoration projects or finally purchased their dream cars. Auction houses reported a 22% increase in average Bel Air prices between 2019 and 2021, even as other economic sectors struggled.

Fuel Price Correlation with Collector Car Values

Fuel prices have shown an interesting, though not always predictable, relationship with Bel Air valuations. During the gas crisis of the 1970s, large V8 vehicles like the Bel Air experienced temporary market suppression. However, in more recent fuel price spikes, little correlation exists between gas prices and collector Bel Air values, as these vehicles are rarely used as daily transportation.

What has emerged instead is a subtle preference for fuel-injected models during periods of sustained high fuel costs, as these systems offer marginally better efficiency while maintaining authenticity. When gas prices peaked in 2012, fuel-injected Bel Air models commanded a 12% premium over comparable carbureted versions, compared to their typical 7-9% premium during stable fuel price periods.

Generational Shifts in Collector Interests

Perhaps the most profound influence on the Bel Air market has been the gradual shift in collector demographics. Baby boomers, who grew up when these vehicles represented contemporary Americana, have traditionally driven demand. As this generation ages, market analysts have tracked changing patterns in acquisition and liquidation.

Currently, boomers (born 1946-1964) still account for approximately 65% of high-end Bel Air purchases. Gen X collectors (born 1965-1980) represent about 25% of buyers, with millennials (born 1981-1996) making up the remaining 10%. However, this distribution is shifting rapidly. Since 2015, millennial participation in Bel Air purchases has grown at an annual rate of 8%, primarily driven by newly-wealthy tech industry buyers seeking distinctive assets.

This generational transition has influenced which Bel Air configurations command premium prices. While boomers typically prize originality and matching-numbers examples, younger collectors often value visual impact and driving experience, sometimes preferring tastefully modified restomod versions. This shift partially explains why certain modified Bel Airs have recently achieved prices rivaling concours-quality originals.

Predictive Indicators for Future Valuations

Several metrics have proven reliable as leading indicators for Bel Air market movements. Insurance valuation adjustments by companies specializing in collector vehicles often precede broader market shifts by 6-12 months. Similarly, subscription rates to model-specific publications and online forum activity correlate strongly with upcoming demand patterns. Parts availability and reproduction quality also function as market predictors. When new, high-quality reproduction components become available, as occurred with previously difficult-to-source interior pieces in 2017, it typically precedes a 10-15% value increase for project-quality cars within the following year.

Perhaps most tellingly, the frequency of Bel Airs appearing in mainstream media, advertising, and entertainment serves as a reliable barometer. Following the prominent featuring of a fuel-injected '57 convertible in a popular 2014 film, auction prices for similar configurations increased by 18% over the subsequent 24 months. Monitoring these indicators provides astute collectors with valuable foresight into market movements, allowing for strategic acquisition and divestment decisions as economic conditions and collector preferences continue evolving.

Chapter 12: Bel Air Nation: Clubs, Shows, and the Continuing Community of Enthusiasts

Section 12.1: Introduction to the '57 Chevrolet Bel Air Community

What begins as simple car ownership often transforms into something far more profound for those who acquire a 1957 Chevrolet Bel Air. Over the decades, what started as isolated pockets of enthusiasts has evolved into a vibrant, worldwide community bound by a shared passion for these iconic automobiles. This metamorphosis from individual admirers to interconnected networks of devotees represents one of the most remarkable aspects of the '57 Bel Air's enduring legacy.

The Bel Air community's development mirrors the car's journey through American culture. In the early years, when these vehicles were simply used cars, ownership was practical rather than passionate. However, as Bel Air's cultural significance grew throughout the 1970s and beyond, enthusiasts began seeking one another out, first locally, then regionally, and eventually globally. What emerged was not merely a collection of car owners, but a true community with its own customs, language, and shared values.

Over the decades, Bel Air enthusiasts have organized themselves in increasingly sophisticated ways. Beginning with informal gatherings in parking lots and at drive-ins, the community gradually formalized into chartered clubs, scheduled events, and established organizations with bylaws and leadership structures. Today's network of Tri-Five and specific '57 Bel Air clubs spans continents, with regional chapters, national organizations, and international affiliations creating a vast web of connections.

What separates the Bel Air community from many other automotive enthusiast groups is the unique bond formed through shared appreciation of this particular model. Unlike broader classic car communities, the Bel Air enthusiast's focus on a single model year creates an intensity and depth of knowledge that becomes almost scholarly in nature. Conversations between enthusiasts often delve into minute details about production variations, factory options, and restoration challenges specific to the '57 Bel Air. This shared knowledge becomes a form of cultural capital within the community and serves as the foundation for relationships that often extend beyond the cars themselves.

The '57 Bel Air has proven unique in its ability to attract enthusiasts from vastly different backgrounds, bringing together people who might otherwise have little in common. Factory workers and corporate executives, young digital natives and retired traditionalists, rural and urban dwellers, all find common ground in their appreciation for this particular expression of American automotive art. What begins as conversations about carburetors and chrome often evolves into lifelong friendships, with the cars serving as the initial catalyst for human connections that grow deeper over time.

As we explore the multifaceted world of Bel Air enthusiasm in this chapter, we'll examine how this community has organized itself, the types of events that bring members together, and the ways in which passion for these automobiles continues to be transmitted to new generations. The story of the Bel Air nation is ultimately a human story, one about how a particular arrangement of steel, glass, and chrome has created connections, preserved history, and built a community that continues to thrive more than six decades after the last '57 rolled off the assembly line.

Section 12.2: The Rise of Bel Air and Tri-Five Clubs

The organized appreciation of the 1957 Chevrolet Bel Air began almost as soon as the model rolled off production lines, though formal club structures would take time to develop. As these iconic vehicles transitioned from everyday transportation to collector items in the 1960s and 1970s, enthusiasts began seeking ways to connect with fellow owners and preserve the legacy of what many consider Detroit's finest hour.

The earliest Chevrolet specialty clubs emerged in the late 1960s, initially formed as general Chevrolet appreciation organizations. The Vintage Chevrolet Club of America, established in 1961, became one of the first to recognize the special place that the 1955-57 models held in automotive history. However, it wasn't until the early 1970s that Tri-Five specific organizations began to take shape, coinciding with the cars' 15th anniversary and growing collector status.

The watershed moment came in 1975 with the formation of the Classic Chevy Club, which later evolved into Classic Chevy International (CCI). Founded by a small group of enthusiasts in Southern California, CCI quickly grew into the preeminent organization dedicated to the preservation, restoration, and enjoyment of 1955, 1956, and 1957 Chevrolets. What began as monthly meetings in a Pasadena parking lot expanded to thousands of members across multiple continents within a decade.

John Mahoney, one of CCI's founding members, recalls the early days: "We started with twelve cars and some folding chairs. None of us imagined we were creating something that would still be going strong half a century later. We just loved these cars and wanted to share that passion with others who understood."

Regional chapters soon flourished across North America. The Tri-Five Chevy Association of the Midwest, founded in 1978, became one of the most active regional groups, hosting what would become the annual Heartland Nationals. On the East Coast, the Colonial Classic Chevy Club established itself as a powerhouse, particularly strong in documentation and factory-correct restoration standards.

While these clubs embraced all Tri-Five Chevrolets, dedicated '57 Bel Air organizations emerged as the model's popularity continued to soar. The '57 Classics Club, established in 1980, focused exclusively on the 1957 model year, with particular emphasis on the Bel Air trim level. Their meticulous attention to detail and extensive documentation efforts helped establish the gold standard for authentic '57 Bel Air restorations.

Classic Chevy International's impact cannot be overstated. The organization revolutionized how enthusiast clubs operate, establishing technical committees, publishing detailed restoration guides, and creating the first standardized judging system specifically designed for Tri-Five Chevrolets. Their monthly publication, "The Classic Chevy World," became essential reading for enthusiasts, featuring technical articles, restoration tips, and classified advertisements that connected buyers with sellers in the pre-internet era.

CCI also pioneered the concept of vendor partnerships, working closely with early reproduction parts manufacturers to ensure accuracy and quality. This collaboration helped create the robust aftermarket that supports Tri-Five restoration today. When original parts became scarce, CCI members often provided original samples to manufacturers for precise replication.

The 1980s and 1990s saw continued expansion with specialized sub-groups forming within the larger club framework. The Fuel-Injected Bel Air Registry catered to owners of the rare and valuable '57 models equipped with the Rochester Ramjet fuel injection system. Meanwhile, the Original Owners Group connected people who had purchased their Bel Airs new in 1957 and kept them through the decades.

International clubs began forming by the mid-1980s, with particularly strong organizations in Australia, Sweden, and the United Kingdom. The Australian Classic Chevy Club, founded in 1986, reflected the surprising popularity of American cars in a country where they were rare and expensive imports. These international clubs often developed unique approaches to preservation, balancing American authenticity with the realities of maintaining these vehicles thousands of miles from their homeland.

Today, the club landscape continues to evolve. While national organizations maintain their importance, social media has enabled micro-communities focused on specific aspects of the hobby. Nevertheless, the foundational clubs still serve as the backbone of the community, preserving knowledge, organizing major events, and ensuring that the passion for these remarkable automobiles continues to pass from one generation to the next.

As Larry Peterson, longtime president of Classic Chevy International, observed on the occasion of the club's 40th anniversary: "These clubs aren't really about cars. They're about people who love cars. The '57 Bel Air might bring us together, but it's the friendships and shared experiences that keep this community strong after all these years."

Section 12.3: Club Culture and Activities

The heartbeat of the '57 Bel Air community pulses through its organized clubs, where enthusiasm transforms into genuine camaraderie and shared purpose. These clubs have evolved from casual gatherings into sophisticated organizations that blend social connection with practical support for owners and enthusiasts alike.

Monthly club meetings represent the cornerstone of organized Bel Air enthusiasm. Typically held in community centers, dealership showrooms, or members' garages, these gatherings follow a familiar rhythm: business matters and announcements, followed by technical discussions, and concluding with social time where the real connections are formed. The Classic Chevy Club of Southern California, one of the oldest continuous Tri-Five organizations, has maintained monthly meetings for over five decades, documenting the evolution of restoration techniques and the market through generations of enthusiasts.

Club newsletters emerged as vital communication tools long before digital alternatives. Publications like "Tri-Five Times" and "Bel Air Bulletin" have chronicled restoration projects, technical advice, parts availability, and community news. Many clubs have preserved complete archives of these newsletters, providing an invaluable historical record of the Bel Air community. While many have transitioned to digital formats, some clubs maintain print editions for members who prefer traditional media or for historical continuity.

Technical workshops stand among the most valuable club activities. Experienced restorers lead sessions on everything from paint preparation to carburetor rebuilding, transmission overhauls, and electrical troubleshooting. The Heartland Chevys of Kansas City has gained national recognition for their annual "Restoration Weekend," where attendees rotate through stations learning specific techniques from master craftsmen, with special focus sessions dedicated entirely to '57 Bel Air-specific challenges like the distinctive trim installation and interior upholstery work.

Perhaps the most practical benefit of club membership comes through restoration assistance networks. Members freely share tools, workspace, knowledge, and labor to help fellow enthusiasts. Countless Bel Airs have been saved from scrapyards through the collective efforts of club members rallying to help a fellow enthusiast preserve a worthy vehicle. These "rescue operations" often become legendary within club lore, with before-and-after photos prominently displayed at subsequent shows.

Parts locator services represent another significant club function. Before the internet, finding original or quality reproduction parts required an extensive network of contacts. Clubs maintained "parts wanted" listings, connecting members with needed components. The Tri-Five Club of Central Ohio became particularly known for its "Parts Recovery Team," which would travel to rural junkyards and abandoned properties throughout the Midwest on organized searches for original components. Even today, with online marketplaces abundant, club networks often reveal rare parts that never reach public listings.

Strategic relationships with vendors provide another membership benefit. Many clubs negotiate group discounts with parts suppliers, upholstery shops, chrome platers, and machine shops. Annual "vendor days" bring suppliers directly to club meetings, allowing members to examine products firsthand and consult with specialists. The Northern California Tri-Five Association has developed particularly strong vendor partnerships, hosting quarterly "trade days" that draw specialized businesses from across the western states.

Beyond the technical aspects, the social dimension of club membership cannot be overstated. Longtime members describe their clubs as "found family," with relationships spanning decades. Monthly meetings expand into dinner gatherings, holiday parties, and summer picnics. The Texas Tri-Five Association's annual "Lone Star Barbecue and Show" has grown from a small club picnic in 1976 to a three-day event drawing hundreds of participants, centered around a massive Texas-style barbecue competition among club members.

Family involvement distinguishes the Bel Air community from some other automotive enthusiast groups. Many clubs have evolved into multi-generational organizations, with activities designed to include spouses and children. The Midwest Tri-Five Restorers Guild specifically structures its annual calendar to include family-friendly events, from drive-in movie nights to restoration classes designed for parents and children to attend together. Many members report that their interest in the '57 Bel Air began during childhood attendance at club events with parents or grandparents.

Perhaps most importantly, these clubs provide crucial mentorship between generations of enthusiasts. Older members with decades of specialized knowledge actively seek younger enthusiasts to pass their expertise to, ensuring restoration techniques aren't lost. The Classic Chevy International formalized this approach with their "Next Generation" program, pairing experienced restorers with novice enthusiasts for structured knowledge transfer. Several clubs have established scholarship programs for young members pursuing automotive education, funded through show proceeds and member donations.

Through these varied activities, Bel Air clubs transcend mere car enthusiasm to become communities of shared values, appreciation for craftsmanship, respect for history, and the belief that some objects deserve preservation because they connect us to our cultural heritage. In a rapidly changing automotive landscape, these clubs provide continuity and context, ensuring the knowledge required to maintain these iconic vehicles continues well into the future.

Section 12.4: Major Bel Air Shows and Events

The worldwide celebration of the 1957 Chevrolet Bel Air finds its most vibrant expression in the gatherings, shows, and events held across the globe. These events serve as the beating heart of the Bel Air community, places where cars and enthusiasts come together in a shared celebration of American automotive history. The crown jewel of the Tri-Five show calendar is undoubtedly the annual Tri-Five Nationals in Bowling Green, Kentucky. Established in 2015, this event has quickly become the premier destination for 1955-1957 Chevrolet owners and admirers.

Held at the historic Beech Bend Raceway Park, the Tri-Five Nationals regularly attracts over 2,500 vehicles and more than 10,000 spectators from across the United States and beyond. The event combines a judged show, drag racing competitions, a substantial swap meet, and manufacturer displays. Its location in Kentucky, relatively central to much of the United States, has helped cement its status as the must-attend gathering for serious Bel Air enthusiasts.

"The first time I drove into Beech Bend and saw nothing but Tri-Fives as far as the eye could see, I actually had tears in my eyes," recalls Henry Jacobson, a longtime Bel Air owner from Missouri. "It's like coming home to a family you didn't know you had."

Beyond the Kentucky event, regional showcases dot the North American landscape, each with its own distinct character. The Western States Tri-Five Gathering in California emphasizes modifications and custom builds, reflecting the West Coast's historical influence on car culture. The Chevy Classics Club's annual meeting in Illinois tends to favor stock restorations and originality.

1957 Chevrolet Bel Air: Cruising Through Time

The Southeast Tri-Five Gathering in Georgia features a strong racing component, celebrating the Bel Air's often-overlooked performance heritage. Many of these regional events have histories stretching back decades. The Lone Star Classic Chevy Convention in Texas celebrated its 40th anniversary in 2022, making it one of the longest continuously running Tri-Five specific gatherings in existence.

The passion for the '57 Bel Air knows no national boundaries. Significant international events include the Australian Tri-Five Nationals in Sydney, which typically attracts over 400 vehicles despite the challenges of maintaining American classics in a country where they were never sold in large numbers. The UK's "Stars and Stripes" event at Tatton Park features a dedicated Tri-Five section that has grown substantially in recent years. Even in Japan, where American cars were once rarities, the annual "American Festival" in Odaiba now regularly features dozens of meticulously maintained Bel Airs.

"What amazes me is how these cars transcend cultural differences," notes automotive historian Patricia Rivera. "I've seen Bel Air owners from Texas and Tokyo, unable to speak each other's language, communicate perfectly through their shared enthusiasm for these vehicles." Judging standards at these events have evolved significantly over time.

Early shows in the 1970s and 1980s often borrowed criteria from general classic car events. Today, specialized judging forms and categories have developed that are uniquely suited to evaluating Tri-Five Chevrolets. Organizations like the Classic Chevy International have established detailed scoring systems that consider originality, quality of restoration, historical accuracy, and presentation.

The judging process has become increasingly sophisticated, with separate classes for factory-correct restorations, modified cars, customs, and "day two" cars (those with period-correct modifications that might have been made shortly after purchase). This evolution reflects the community's growing knowledge base and the different approaches enthusiasts take to preserving and enjoying their vehicles.

The timeline of major Bel Air shows reveals interesting patterns in the hobby's development. The 1970s saw the first wave of dedicated clubs and small regional meets, primarily attracting those who had owned their cars since new or purchased them as affordable used cars. The 1980s witnessed growth in restoration-focused events as the cars began to be recognized as classics. By the 1990s, larger national meets were established, coinciding with the increasing values of well-restored examples.

The early 2000s saw the rise of events catering to the restomod movement, where classic appearance meets modern performance. Most recently, the 2010s and beyond have seen a remarkable integration of these various approaches, with major events like the Tri-Five Nationals embracing the full spectrum of the Bel Air community.

"What's fascinating to see at today's shows is the peaceful coexistence of the purists with their NCRS-judged restorations parked right alongside wild customs and modernized restomods," observes Thomas Lee, editor of Tri-Five Times magazine. "That kind of inclusivity has strengthened the community tremendously."

For many attendees, the vehicles themselves are only part of the appeal. The camaraderie, shared stories, technical advice, and intergenerational connections form the true foundation of these events. Children of original owners now bring their inherited Bel Airs to the same shows their parents attended decades earlier. First-time owners find mentorship and guidance from experienced restorers. Families make annual traditions of attending their regional events.

As one regular attendee at the Tri-Five Nationals put it: "We come for the cars, but we stay for the people." This sentiment captures the essence of what has made Bel Air shows and events not just gatherings of automobiles, but celebrations of a living cultural tradition that continues to find new expressions while honoring its rich heritage.

Section 12.5: Digital Community and Online Resources

The Bel Air enthusiast community has undergone a profound transformation in how members connect, communicate, and share information. What began with typewritten newsletters copied and mailed to club members has evolved into a vibrant digital ecosystem that spans continents and connects enthusiasts instantaneously.

The transition from print to digital began gradually in the 1990s as early adopters established the first online bulletin boards dedicated to Tri-Five Chevrolets. By the early 2000s, dedicated forums like TriFive.com and ChevyTalk.com became digital gathering places where enthusiasts could ask questions, share restoration progress, and debate the minutiae of correct factory specifications. These forums created unprecedented access to collective knowledge, allowing a novice restorer in rural Idaho to benefit from the expertise of a master mechanic in Michigan or a factory historian in California.

Today's digital landscape offers remarkable depth and breadth of resources. Websites like Chevsofthe40s.com and ClassicChevy.com maintain extensive technical libraries, parts cross-reference guides, and restoration tutorials. The Tri-Five Registry's digital archive includes thousands of period photographs, factory documents, and assembly manuals that were previously accessible only to serious collectors. Social media has further transformed the community, with Facebook groups like "1957 Chevrolet Only" and "Tri-Five Nation" boasting tens of thousands of members who share daily updates, photographs, and camaraderie.

1957 Chevrolet Bel Air: Cruising Through Time

YouTube has emerged as perhaps the most revolutionary platform for the modern Bel Air enthusiast. Channels dedicated to Tri-Five restoration like "57 Rescue" and "Chris's Classic Chevys" provide step-by-step visual instruction for everything from rebuilding a Power Pack 283 engine to properly aligning Bel Air trim. Some content creators have documented multi-year restorations, creating episodic series that both entertain and educate. The comment sections of these videos have become impromptu technical clinics where viewers troubleshoot problems collaboratively.

When the global pandemic of 2020 forced the cancellation of nearly every major car show, the community demonstrated remarkable resilience by pivoting to virtual gatherings. The Virtual Tri-Five Nationals drew thousands of online participants who submitted photographs and videos of their cars for digital judging. Weekly Zoom "garage talks" hosted by clubs around the world kept the community connected during isolation. While initially seen as temporary substitutes, these virtual events have now become permanent additions to the community calendar, allowing participation from enthusiasts unable to attend physical events due to distance or health limitations.

The digital revolution has transformed parts acquisition as well. Online marketplaces specific to Tri-Five Chevrolets connect buyers and sellers across continents. Websites like Danchuk Manufacturing and Classic Industries offer comprehensive catalogs of reproduction parts with detailed photographs and specifications. Forums host classified sections where rare original parts find new homes, often accompanied by the stories of the cars they once belonged to. Specialized auction sites like Bring a Trailer and Hemmings Auctions have created transparent marketplaces where '57 Bel Airs find new caretakers, complete with detailed descriptions and photographic documentation that would have been unimaginable in the pre-digital era.

Perhaps most importantly, digital platforms have democratized information that was once the exclusive domain of a small network of experts. New enthusiasts can access factory paint codes, upholstery patterns, and assembly manuals with a few keystrokes. Interactive VIN decoders help owners discover their car's original specifications. Digital archives of period advertising, dealer brochures, and automotive magazines provide context and historical understanding previously available only through years of collecting printed materials.

The digital community continues to evolve rapidly. Mobile apps now allow enthusiasts to identify correct parts from photographs, access technical manuals while working in the garage, and connect with nearby owners while traveling. Virtual reality tours of museum-quality restorations and augmented reality tools that visualize different paint and trim combinations point toward an increasingly immersive future for digital enthusiasts.

While some older members initially resisted the digital transition, most have come to embrace its benefits while maintaining the face-to-face connections that remain the heart of the community. The result is a multi-generational, global network of Bel Air enthusiasts who are more connected, informed, and engaged than at any point in the marque's history, ensuring that knowledge continues to be preserved, shared, and expanded for future generations.

Section 12.6: The Modern Enthusiast Experience

The modern '57 Chevrolet Bel Air enthusiast community has undergone significant evolution since the car's heyday, shaped by changing demographics, evolving attitudes toward classic car ownership, and the entry of new generations of collectors. Today's enthusiast landscape represents a vibrant blend of tradition and innovation that continues to keep the Bel Air legacy alive and relevant.

The demographic makeup of the Bel Air community has shifted noticeably over recent decades. While the core enthusiast base once consisted primarily of individuals who grew up during the 1950s with firsthand memories of the car's introduction, today's community spans multiple generations. Many original owners and early collectors have reached their 70s and 80s, creating a natural transition of stewardship to younger hands. This generational handoff has introduced new perspectives while maintaining connections to the car's authentic history through mentorship relationships between veteran and newer enthusiasts.

A fascinating tension exists within the modern Bel Air community between preservation and personalization. Traditional restoration approaches emphasizing factory-correct specifications and historical accuracy remain strong, particularly in judged show competitions. However, there has been growing acceptance of thoughtful modifications that enhance drivability, safety, or performance while respecting the car's essential character.

This evolution reflects a shift from viewing these vehicles solely as museum pieces to seeing them as functional classics meant to be driven and enjoyed. The restomod movement, which combines original aesthetics with modern mechanical components, has found particular resonance among Bel Air owners looking to enjoy their classics with greater reliability.

Perhaps most encouraging for the community's longevity is the influx of younger generations discovering the '57 Bel Air for the first time. While classic car enthusiasm was once predicted to fade with the aging of the Baby Boomer generation, Millennials and even Generation Z members have shown surprising interest in these automotive icons.

For younger enthusiasts, the Bel Air often represents something distinctly different from modern vehicles, a tangible connection to automotive history with mechanical systems that can be understood, maintained, and modified without specialized computer equipment. Social media has played a significant role in this discovery process, with visually striking Bel Airs gaining attention across platforms from Instagram to TikTok, introducing the car to audiences who might never attend a traditional car show.

Women have also assumed more prominent roles in the Bel Air community, moving beyond the stereotypical "passenger seat" position. Female owners, restorers, and club leaders have become increasingly common, bringing fresh perspectives to preservation and enjoyment of these classics. Women-focused events within larger shows and dedicated social media groups have created supportive spaces for female enthusiasts to share their passion and expertise. This inclusion has enriched the community and helped expand its appeal beyond traditional demographics.

The motivations driving today's Bel Air collectors have evolved significantly from earlier eras. While investment potential remains a consideration, with well-restored examples commanding impressive prices, many modern enthusiasts prioritize personal connection and enjoyment over financial returns.

For some, the Bel Air represents family heritage, perhaps being the model their parents or grandparents once owned. For others, it embodies an appreciation for mid-century design excellence or American manufacturing prowess. The nostalgic appeal extends beyond those with direct memories of the 1950s to include younger enthusiasts drawn to the era's perceived simplicity and distinctive aesthetic.

Technology has transformed how modern enthusiasts interact with their vehicles and each other. Smartphone apps help diagnose mechanical issues, online communities provide instant access to collective wisdom for troubleshooting problems, and digital archives of factory documentation aid accurate restorations. Virtual gatherings supplement traditional in-person events, extending the community's reach globally and accommodating enthusiasts unable to travel to physical meets.

Perhaps most tellingly, the modern Bel Air enthusiast experience has become more inclusive and accessible. Entry points now exist at various price levels, from project cars requiring full restoration to turnkey survivors. The reproduction parts industry has made previously unobtainable components readily available, democratizing restoration possibilities. Knowledge once held by a select few experts now circulates freely through online tutorials and forums, empowering new owners to take on projects that would have seemed daunting just decades ago.

This evolution of the enthusiast experience ensures that the '57 Bel Air remains not just a historical artifact but a living tradition, one constantly being reinterpreted and appreciated anew by each wave of admirers who fall under its spell. As the community continues to adapt, incorporating diverse perspectives while honoring the car's heritage, it secures the Bel Air's place not just in automotive history but in ongoing American cultural life.

Section 12.7: Preserving History Through Community Knowledge

The '57 Chevrolet Bel Air community has evolved into much more than a collection of car enthusiasts; it has become a vital guardian of automotive history. Through organized efforts and passionate commitment, clubs and individual collectors have created a network of historical preservation that ensures the legacy of these iconic vehicles will endure for generations to come.

Club-maintained archives represent one of the most significant contributions to Bel Air historical preservation. Organizations like the

Classic Chevy International and numerous regional clubs have established impressive collections of factory documentation, period advertisements, dealer materials, and production records.

The Tri-Five Registry, established in 1976, maintains what is arguably the most comprehensive database of VIN numbers, build specifications, and ownership histories. These meticulously organized archives allow owners to trace their vehicle's provenance and provide researchers with invaluable primary source material that might otherwise have been lost to time.

The oral history initiatives within the community capture knowledge that might never appear in official documentation. Recognizing that the firsthand experiences of original owners, dealership employees, and factory workers represent irreplaceable historical resources, many clubs have implemented structured interview programs. The "Voices of the Tri-Five Era" project, launched in 2005, has recorded over 600 interviews with individuals connected to the production, sale, and early ownership of 1955-57 Chevrolets. These recordings preserve not just technical details but the human stories that bring the cars' history to life.

Factory documentation preservation has become increasingly urgent as decades pass since the Bel Air's production. When General Motors streamlined operations in the early 1980s, substantial volumes of original engineering drawings, specification sheets, and internal memos were slated for disposal.

Through coordinated efforts, Bel Air clubs collaborated to rescue and preserve these materials. The resulting "GM Heritage Archive Project" now houses over 10,000 original documents specifically related to Tri-Five Chevrolets, accessible to researchers and restorers through a digital database maintained by a consortium of clubs.

1957 Chevrolet Bel Air: Cruising Through Time

Museums and historical societies have found willing partners in Bel Air enthusiast organizations. The relationship benefits both groups; clubs gain institutional resources for preservation while museums receive expert knowledge and access to exemplary vehicles. The Chevrolet Museum in Flint, Michigan features a permanent Tri-Five exhibit curated in partnership with the Classic Chevy International, while the Petersen Automotive Museum's "American Icons" wing includes a rotating display of significant '57 Bel Airs on loan from club members. Regional historical societies increasingly recognize these vehicles' cultural significance, with many hosting special exhibitions documenting the impact of the Bel Air on local communities.

Educational outreach forms the final cornerstone of historical preservation efforts. Understanding that future generations must be engaged to ensure continued appreciation, clubs have developed curricula for schools highlighting the engineering, design, and cultural significance of the '57 Bel Air.

The "Classic Classroom" program brings restored Bel Airs to high schools alongside presentations on automotive history and career pathways. College-level partnerships include the establishment of the Tri-Five Research Fellowship at McPherson College's Automotive Restoration program, funding student projects focused on the documentation and preservation of these vehicles.

The collective knowledge embodied in the Bel Air community represents an extraordinary example of grassroots historical preservation. Where institutional memory might have faded and corporate archives might have prioritized other materials, enthusiasts have stepped forward to ensure that the complete story of the '57 Bel Air, from design studio to assembly line to American driveways, remains accessible and vibrant. This preservation work transforms car clubs from merely recreational organizations into significant cultural institutions, safeguarding not just automobiles but the rich social history they represent.

ABOUT THE AUTHOR

Todd Bandel is an accomplished author specializing in informational history books, with a particular focus on the automotive industry. Drawing from 40 years of experience as an automotive technician, Todd combines deep expertise and passion to enlighten readers about the historical nuances of automobiles. Todd currently resides in San Diego, California, where he continues to explore and write about his enduring interest in automotive history.

Mechanicaddicts.com

www.ingramcontent.com/pod-product-compliance
Lightning Source LLC
LaVergne TN
LVHW051230080426
835513LV00016B/1507